EMERGE!

Upgrade from Existing to Living Your Bold, Fearless, Abundant Life Now

ISBN: 978-0-578-48424-2

This book is dedicated to all the incredible sons and daughters of God who are right at the brink of discovering who you truly are and what you were created for. This is your time to EMERGE! This book is for you!

Table of Contents

1. EMERGE
IN YOUR IDENTITY

Tiffany Bethea

In Genesis 1:26-27 God said, "**26** *And God said, Let us make man in our image, after our likeness: and let them have dominion over the fish of the sea, and over the fowl of the air, and over the cattle, and over all the earth, and over every creeping thing that creepeth upon the earth. 27 So God created man in his own image, in the image of God created he him; male and female created he them.*

I don't know if you are like me, but I've heard this passage of scripture about a million times since childhood. Typically while hearing about the creation story this comes up. Yet, as familiar as this passage is I often wonder if we truly understand the significance. The God who created the universe all by himself, who put the stars in place and who separated like from darkness made us in His likeness. The same God who created multiple galaxies, planets, put life in something as small as a gnat and orchestrated the four seasons made you just like him.

We are made in God's image and likeness meaning that we are copies of Him, we are His sons and daughters and we have some of his traits. This is easy for all of the parents to grasp because our children are made in our image and likeness. It always amazes me to see my son make a facial expression that I make or do something that I haven't intentionally taught him but just by the fact of him having my genes there is some me in him. It is the same with us and God. We have some of His characteristics inside of us. But not enough of us live like we do.

As a worship leader, I often lead people in songs that say things like "My God is big" or "Our God is greater" or "What a mighty God we serve", but yet we haven't made the connection that all of the wonderful things we ascribe about God related to us as well. We revere God as though He is awesome, powerful, great, majestic and yet we don't often esteem ourselves the same way.

Now I want you to understand that I'm in no way suggesting that we see ourselves as God. I have had seasons of life where I thought I was big and bad enough to be God and to run my own life without Him. That didn't go so well! I'm simply speaking of fully understanding who we are so that we can walk out the plan of God for our lives.

John 10:10 tells us that "The thief cometh not, but for to steal, and to kill, and to destroy: I have come that they might have life and that they might have it more abundantly." Jesus came that we would live an abundant, flourishing life but he was very transparent in letting us know that the enemy also has an agenda to ensure that we would not experience that life. Sometimes we really give the enemy too much power. The reality is that He cannot take anything from us or cause us to miss God's plans but he can use tactics to make us walk away or not even pursue it at all. One of the biggest tricks of the enemy that He uses is an identity crisis. If He can lie to us enough to make us forget that we are God's children and made in His image, we will forget the power we have and never tap into it. Too many believers live this way today.

One of the books that has massively impacted my life is Outwitting the Devil by Napoleon Hill. Hill originally wrote this book in 1938 but the book was only released after his death for fear of the backlash it would have received. In this book, he vividly describes a conversation that he has with the enemy where all of his strategies and tactics for destroying people's lives are revealed. If you haven't read this book it is one I highly encourage. It is one of those books where are you read it you won't be the same.

In the book, he talks about something called drifting. Drifting is a tactic used to keep people from living a purposeful and abundant life as God desires. During the interview, Hill asks the enemy to describe someone who has become a drifter. The answer is given as someone who lacks a major purpose in life and someone who lacks confidence. Because of these two simple things he stresses that this person is not likely to accomplish anything in life. They are simply drifting along. The person that they describe as a drifter in the book is someone who is suffering from the identity crisis. They are someone who simply doesn't live in the reality of all they are and all that they possess.

Let's be honest for a moment, how many people do you know that lives this way? Do you live this way? It is my desire that in this chapter and throughout this book that you gain the revelation and tools to break free from drifting and any identity crisis and step into the fullness of all that God has created you to be. It is my hope that you will tap into the power and Holy Spirit that lives inside of you and harness it for more than Sunday service shouting, but rather for guidance and wisdom. You are created to conquer, to reign and experience a passionate, fulfilling and abundant life. But in order to do so, you must know who you are and whose you are. Let's look at some of the things that shape our identity:

3

OUR EXPERIENCES

One of the biggest things that impacts how we see ourselves is what we have experienced in our lives. No matter how much we see scriptures about how awesome God is if we have lived a life full of disappointment, struggle, heartache we allow those things to tell us that is who we are. God can try to speak to us and tell us about where He wants to take us in the future but our past tends to set the bar for our achievement and capacity. I don't care what you have experienced in your past you must make 2 Corinthians 5:17 a reality. *"Therefore if any man is in Christ, he is a new creature: old things are passed away; behold, all things have become new."*

You may have experienced struggle, family trauma, disappointment, heartache but they do not define who you are! They are a part of your story but they are not your identity! Because you were born to parents who struggled financially doesn't mean that you cannot live a life of wealth and abundance. Because your parents were divorced when you were a kid or never married at all doesn't mean that you cannot have a happy kingdom marriage. Because no one in your neighborhood or family went to college or started a business doesn't mean that you cannot achieve that. One thing I know about God is that He uses everything for our purpose. You may not be so happy about the negative experiences you've had but I dare you to watch how God will use them for your good. Watch how God will turn it to enhance your life assignment. Don't despise any of your experiences. Don't allow the path you have been allowed by God to journey tell you who you are.

OUR RELATIONSHIPS

No one else can be an open door to discouragement and distraction from the enemy quite like close family and friends. Often times they mean well but it is easy for our identity to get lost in the family we belong to and the circle of friends we have chosen. Many people limit their potential simply based on what the family pattern has been. If no one in the family has done what we see in our mind we think that we aren't able to achieve it either. If everyone in the family has gone to school and gotten a good government job and God is speaking to us to be an entrepreneur, often we question it. What will the family say? Will they understand? Will they tell me to get a "real job"? And so we start on the journey and when it gets rough we think it is a sign this isn't for us instead of persevering to get to the other side.

One of the tough things about family relationships is sometimes stepping back and evaluating. We think that just because people are family or close friends that we have to take their advice. But if they have not walked out the plan of God in their own lives are they really qualified to speak on yours? I don't care if it is your mother or your very best friend. How can they advise you on something they have not done? I'm not talking about being judgmental either because everyone is entitled to their own journey and as long as they are here God is still doing a work in them. But sometimes it's as simple as understanding people can't give directions to where they've never been. If I've never been to your house I can't give someone directions there. Doesn't make me a bad person. Doesn't mean I can't give other advice. But on this topic, I am not well-informed enough. It is the same with our loved ones. We have to weigh the validity and ask ourselves if what they are sharing aligns with God's word and quite frankly if it has worked well for them. If they are living a purposeful passionate life in the plan of God we should definitely consider what they say about our purpose. But if they have not yet made it to that place we have to be careful not to let their words distract us from what God has said about us.

We must be careful not to choose an identity crisis by association. Just because we share a last name, or a circle of friends doesn't mean we have to choose the same life direction. Understand that regardless of what others around you have done, you must make a bold choice for yourself to be exactly who created you to be and live the life he designed for you.

5

So what does it mean to be made in the image of God? How do we grasp our divine identity and live in it?

YOU HAVE DOMINION

"And God said, Let us make man in our image, after our likeness: and let them have dominion" Genesis 1:26. God made it clear during our creation that we are to have dominion, sovereignty or control. He has given us earth as the jurisdiction over which we have control. Do you know what this means? It means you have power and you are in charge! It means that life doesn't get to just throw whatever at you. You get to decide. You may be wondering well how do I do that? Well God showed us in the beginning how we were to operate. If you read Genesis 1&2 and look at how God formed the world, he didn't lift a finger, he simply used His words. Guess what? You have that same power to speak into the atmosphere and create. In fact, the life you live right now is a result of what you have been speaking and forming. Now that will be good news for some and not so good news for others but the encouraging thing is now that you know, you can begin to be intentional about what you speak. How will you use your words to form your world? Don't let life tell you what will happen. You have been given dominion. Use it! Tell life what to do and how to line up with what God said concerning you.

YOU ARE CREATED TO BE FRUITFUL

The instruction to "be fruitful and multiply" in Genesis 1:28 was not just an instruction to have children and populate the earth. It was also an instruction to produce fruit, be productive and take the seeds God has placed in us to manifest and create. Think about it this way everything else that God gave seed to is reproducing after its kind. Apple seeds are producing apples. Pear seeds are producing pears. I have news for you, you haven't only been given egg and seed to produce new humans. You have been given seeds of innovation, creativity, answers, talents, and abilities. It's is God's desire to see you take those seeds and be fruitful. Look at the parable of the talents in Matthew 25:14-30.

The story tells of a ruler who is preparing to travel so he disperses of talents (which is monetary currency) before he goes. When he returns each one accounts for what they have done with theirs. One reports that he hid it in the ground and didn't multiply it at all. God responds and calls him a wicked and slothful servant. God tells him that he should have taken it to the exchangers and had an increase.

Let me ask you a question, are you living a fruitful life? Have you taken the seeds that God has invested in you and multiplied it or is it buried inside of you? You are created to birth ideas and to make an impact on the earth. Don't fall into the trick of drifting through life and living a fruitless, unproductive life. That is not who you were created to be. I don't care who around you lives like that. I don't care if it has been your norm. God's word lets you know that there is another vision for you.

YOU ARE ABUNDANCE

One of the biggest myths that God had to destroy for me was that He has abundance. Instead, He had to reveal to me that He IS abundance. Because of a particular season in my life, I had gotten used to struggle and began to normalize it. God had to remind me that I serve a God who is abundance. He is more than enough and because I am made in His image, I am made from abundance and more than enough. That tells me that I don't have to go through life "chasing paper" or trying to "secure the bag" because abundance is my birthright. If I truly seek the kingdom and all His righteousness, everything I need will be attracted to me. It is not a result of what I do, it is a result of who I am. Do you receive that for yourself? You are made from abundance. You are created for a flourishing life of more than enough. And I want to you realize that I am not just speaking financially. In every area of your life, you are created for prosperity and plenty. You are designed to have a passionate

Emerge In Your Identity

spiritual relationship, strong mental health, physical fitness and nutrition, financial wealth, relational wellness and life in purpose.

Wouldn't it be strange to see a rich man's child living on the street? Wouldn't it be strange to see a person who has a working car in the driveway go ride the bus? Absolutely because you know they have access to more. Well I have good news for you, so do you! Your heavenly father owns it all. Don't let the enemy convince you of anything different. Don't settle for a life of struggle or not enough because you do not know who you are.

As you read the rest of this book allow God to show you how to walk in your true identity and emerge in every area of your life. It is time for you to upgrade from existence to living a bold, fearless and abundant life. Are you ready for more? If so read on for more powerful nuggets and insights from my incredible co-authors.

TIFFANY BETHEA

Tiffany Bethea is a bestselling author, international speaker, trained coach and consultant, ordained minister and mompreneur. She is the founder of Kingdomboss through which she has provided a space for Christian entrepreneurs to build profitable, Christ-centered brands. Through the signature program Kingdomboss Society new and emerging authors, speakers and entrepreneurs mastermind with other believers in business and gain the accountability, resources and strategy they need to be successful. She is also a spiritual teacher and coach who works with millennials on upgrading from their counterfeit existence to truly living the life God has predestined for them. She is passionate about helping people discover their true identity and maximize their potential.

Website:
www.tiffanybethea.com

9

Emerge In Your Identity

2. EMERGE

IN YOUR SPIRIT: BREAK FREE FROM YOUR C.H.A.I.N.S.

Antoine Garrett

Have you ever felt like there was something holding you back? Perhaps you are among those that feel like "there has to be more to life than *this*?!" Maybe you are struggling to reconcile the reality of your current life experiences with the vision you once held for the life you dreamt of. These internal inquiries underline a growing trend amongst people that are feeling stuck. While many people experience these feelings intermittently, there are individuals who struggle with these sentiments with increasing regularity. Some find themselves stuck in the same space day after day, month after month or year after year. People are often held hostage by these strongholds, or limiting beliefs. There are ongoing battles in their minds to break free from the C.H.A.I.N.S. of mental and spiritual bondage.

Break Free From Your C.H.A.I.N.S.
I believe these chains, have several "links" or thought patterns, which hold us captive. In order to break free, we need to examine the five links of bondage and develop strategies for release so we can *EMERGE* victoriously. Each link, which makes up the C.H.A.I.N.S. that keep us bound, was developed and strengthened through the course of our life experiences. We must also discuss empowerment strategies to live free and resist the cycle of victimization. The five links in the C.H.A.I.N.S. which we struggle with are:

<u>COMPARISON. HISTORY. ANXIETY. INSECURITIES.</u>
<u>NEGATIVITY. SIN.</u>

When considering the links that make up our C.H.A.I.N.S we must be open to exploring some difficult spaces. It's often said that we can't heal in spaces that we don't want to deal with. To that end, I believe that it's necessary to define the C.H.A.I.N.S that have us bound. Which issues are impacting you and when did you become entangled? What event or episode in your life created an opening for the chain to become affixed to you. We have to be real about our "stuff" if we are serious about deliverance. We have to do the work of freeing ourselves.

Link #1: COMPARISON

Theodore Roosevelt called comparison "The thief of Joy." The first link, Comparison, is a struggle that has occurred in the lives of people throughout history. In Social Comparison Theory, psychologists suggest that we make comparisons as a way of evaluating ourselves. Our comparison targets, as scientists refer to them, are those we most closely identify with and those in our personal orbit. This research helps us understand why we've measured ourselves against others when dealing with attributes such as appearance, wealth, relationships, achievements or goals. Yet in recent years, this notion of comparison has received an incredible boost with the spread of the internet and social media. We are constantly flooded with images from our peers and celebrities, the person next door and the complete stranger. While the internet has many benefits, the never-ending onslaught of access to the "highlight reel" that others post, is a trap that seems inescapable. We scroll through our timeline and we are tempted to look at others living their best life, and secretly compare our existence to that of our former high school classmates, relatives, coworkers, and others in our social circles.

This Comparison Trap can make you think your best won't ever be good enough. This results in stress and discontentment with life. According to University of Houston psychologist Mai-Ly Nguyen, individuals are likely to feel "discouraged and defeated" by overexposure to social media, which is almost perfectly constructed to make users feel inadequate.

STRATEGIES TO AVOID THE COMPARISON TRAP

- ***Remind yourself that everything that glitters isn't gold.*** This is helpful because we are reminded about the danger of using someone's outward appearance as the totality of their real-life experience. Social media profiles are carefully selected versions of their lives, complete with special filters and picture angles to give the best impression.
- ***Men Lie; Women Lie and Numbers mean nothing.*** Don't allow the hype of likes and followers to sway your views. The number of Twitter followers, Instagram "hearts", LinkedIn connections, or Facebook likes don't sanction a person's value in the world. Society has allowed artificial validation to determine who is to be celebrated and recognized.
- ***Know your triggers.*** It's key to identify the environment where you are most likely to find yourself in the comparison trap. Are you scrolling on social media when you have "downtime" or do you find yourself looking at #relationshipgoals when you're arguing with your spouse or feeling lonely? Be mindful of your thoughts and when

they occur as a means of protecting your emotions and spirit.

- **Count your blessings.** Focus on the many ways you've been blessed you minimize the temptation to look outward. Keeping your thoughts on God, and all that He's seen fit to place in our lives reduces the urge to measure yourself against someone else.
- **Scripture Support to Break free from Comparison:** *Romans 12:4; Ephesians 4: 23-24*

Link #2: HABITS

Typically when we think of habits, we think in terms of "good" (exercising) and "bad" (biting nails). In truth, habits are simply patterns of behavior that are difficult to change. Those patterns can be developed through social conditioning where we learn to accept and expect certain conditions, and we respond accordingly. Our responses can become so natural that we may not even realize when the habit is hindering or limiting us. Understanding the formulation of those patterns and habits is the beginning of freedom from the grip that holds us captive. It's important to look at the routines we follow and the triggers we respond to.

It's often stated that it takes 21 days to form a new habit. While the science on that is not exactly in alignment, there is research done by Phillipa Lally, who suggests it takes more than 2 months before a new behavior becomes automatic — 66 days to be exact. Habit forming can vary widely depending on the behavior, the person, and the circumstances. In Lally's study, it took anywhere from 18 days to 254 days for people to form a new habit. Doing something repetitively over the course of time becomes a habit that we are likely to engage in, often without giving it much thought because it's *"just what I do."* It's also critical to understand the trigger or preceding factor that resulted in the behavior. There may be certain circumstances that elicit predictable responses.

STRATEGIES TO BREAK HABITS

- *Define the behavior you want to change.* Getting more exercise sounds great but it is also vague. You need to think of specific behaviors — going for a half-hour run 3 days a week. Break it down to specific and realistic behaviors that you want to do differently.
- *Identify the triggers.* Recognize the circumstances that are present when you typically grab the ice cream from the refrigerator when you're not really hungry. Be clear about what brought on stress, anger, fear or frustration. By identifying your triggers, you have a way of resisting the urge to do something without thinking about the consequences.
- *Take away the triggers.* We seek to break free from these patterns and we must do something about the triggers themselves. We must be proactive- get the ice cream out of the house, leave the house or work at a different time so you aren't stressed in traffic, or even do a few minutes of deep breathing to relax.
- *Develop a new plan.* Breaking habits isn't about stopping, but substituting. Create a system for managing the situations and have a proactive method of choosing another option. This helps to shift your perspective and direct your action on a new path.
- *Scriptural Support to Break free from Habits*: Ephesians 4:23-24; Romans 12:2

Link #3: ANXIETY

Anxiety is defined as "a feeling of worry, nervousness, or unease, typically about an imminent event or something with an uncertain outcome." Anxiety is a very real feeling about something that has yet to occur. This link impacts a person's everyday functioning. There is a sense of running on a mental, emotional and spiritual treadmill- exhausted by events that have yet to occur. The anxious person thinks "What if? What now?" and the response they imagine is almost always negative. When you feel frightened or seriously

15

Break Free From Your C.H.A.I.N.S.

anxious, your mind is working overtime and you could also feel physical effects. You may have a nagging sense of fear, you may be irritable, have trouble sleeping, develop headaches, or have trouble getting work done and you might even lose self-confidence.

STRATEGIES TO OVERCOME ANXIETY

- ***Check the facts.*** What should you do when your brain makes a mountain out of a molehill? Challenge it. FACTS over Feelings. Focusing on the concrete facts of a situation allows the person to redirect their thoughts around reality and address the actual issue rather than the feeling.
- ***Change the question.*** When you catch yourself asking questions that begin with "What if..." change your question to a statement and then challenge it. "What if the relationship doesn't work out?" is ambiguous and dependent on any number of factors. Change the question to a statement—"I am going to do my part to create a healthy relationship by..."—and include specific steps that are within your realm of influence.
- ***Stay here.*** One way to combat anxiety over what's ahead is to focus on the now. Take a moment to focus on three things that you see around you. Then pay attention to what you three things that you hear. Being acutely aware of your current circumstance helps to reject future fret by allowing you to ground your thoughts in the moment.
- ***Scriptural Support to Overcome Anxiety:*** Matthew 6: 25-27; Philippians 4: 6-7

Link #4: INSECURITY

Insecurity is a lack of confidence or uncertainty about yourself. A sense that somehow you are not enough, in some area of life. The Insecurity link may have different causes. Some individuals were raised in a chaotic environment that kept you constantly guessing. Perhaps you felt overshadowed or outperformed by a sibling, or

16

coworker. Maybe you are recently divorced or have been laid off. You might suffer from a poor body image or awkward social skills. While common occurrences can create insecurities in anyone, the resulting feeling can be displayed in a myriad of ways. An insecure person may steer clear of interacting with others, and avoid contact when they see someone they know in a crowd. Sometimes an insecure person may act like they have no imperfections at all. Insecurity creates people pleasers and crowd followers. An insecure person would rather be liked than be authentic.

STRATEGIES TO DEFEAT INSECURITY

- **List your good qualities.** This may sound easier than it actually is. Take the time to write out everything that makes you feel good about yourself. If that is challenging, asking for feedback from people that you *trust* could be a starting point. In addition to good qualities, keep a record of accomplishments and successes. Journaling about your qualities and successes will provide a tangible reference list for encouragement.
- **Examine your circle.** If you are surrounded by uber-competitive people that consistently create uncomfortable circumstances, perhaps a change of social circle is in order. You don't have to stay connected to toxic people.
- **Find the root.** Be transparent about the origin of your insecurities. Once you've identified the source, the next step is to create a plan to address those hurts and move beyond your safety zone. This may require the guidance of a counselor or therapist- but is work that will change your life in a positive manner.
- **Scriptural Support to Free yourself from Insecurities:** Psalm 139:14; 1 Samuel 16:7

17

Link #5 NEGATIVITY

Proverbs 23: 7 says, *"As a man thinketh in his heart, so is he."* I saw a motivational quote that reads, "Mindset is everything." These two statements are in sync as it relates to the ability of our thinking-positive or negative to guide our lives. It would be great to say that we are positive *all* the time. However, the reality is that we all face moments of difficulty when it is extremely challenging to remain upbeat. Addressing the link of Negativity isn't dealing with occasionally challenged thinking. This consistent thought pattern becomes disruptive when the outlook is negative. If unchecked, a negative outlook can overtake a person's life and wreak havoc. It is part of the fear-flight mechanism in which the brain uses most of its neurons to keep up with all the bad news that is stored in the memory. Positive people develop the ability to evaluate and counteract this mechanism. The negative person is always worried and pessimistic. A negative person thinks the whole world is against them. Being negative can impact people around us if we drain the positive air out of the environment with our hyper-negativity.

STRATEGIES TO END NEGATIVITY

- ***Change your diet.*** Limit the amount of negativity you consume in music, social media, and conversation. By constructing boundaries, you allow yourself the freedom from the negative voices that you have been accustomed to welcoming and echoing.
- ***Count your blessings.*** Literally, pause daily to reflect on all the things that God has done for you. Create a list. Write as many things as you can think about in a one-minute timed reflection period. Don't evaluate what you've written, simply write. Force your thinking to focus on positive. There may be one item on the first day, but keep doing it until you still have things to write when your timer goes off. Do this as often as you feel negativity starting to creep up on you.

- *Words have power.* The way you speak reinforces what you think. Challenge yourself to refrain from using the word "but." The Bible reminds us in Proverbs 18:21, "That the power of life and death is in the tongue." Remember, words create actions- good and bad. We must realize that we have more influence on our circumstances simply by what we say.

- *Scriptural Support to overpower Negativity:* Philippians 4:8; Proverbs 15:4

Link #6 SIN

The final link in the C.H.A.I.N.S. that hold us captive is Sin. The Bible defines sin as the breaking, or transgression, of God's law (1 John 3:4). It is also described as disobedience or rebellion against God (Deuteronomy 9:7), as well as independence from God. The original translation means "to miss the mark" of God's holy standard of righteousness. The Bible is filled with examples of sin. From Adam & Eve to King David and even Judas that missed the mark. But missing the mark isn't exclusive to the Bible. You and I struggle with the final link, Sin, on a daily basis.

Much is written in the Bible about our need to forgive those who transgress against us. We've been told that one way to get over a past wrong is to forgive the perpetrator. But what if you're the one to blame? What if the misdeeds you're having a hard time moving past are ones *you're* responsible for? It's difficult to forgive ourselves. Perhaps sin holds us through the accompanying guilt or shame that follows our actions. A spirit of condemnation convinces us that our past actions have disqualified us from God's provision. While there may be no way to "undo" past mistakes, we can make change our thinking about our sin.

Strategies to be released from the power of Sin

19

Break Free From Your C.H.A.I.N.S.

- *Repair the damages.* One way to address a hurt you caused is to ask what you could do to make up for the past. This could positively impact the person/people we hurt.
- *Get out of your head.* Giving past failures less time and attention is one way to help move forward. You could also examine the expectations and standards you hold for yourself. You could write yourself a letter, or take a self-imposed break to process your feelings. Put time into this and decide that when you are done, you'll really let it go.
- *Commit to Caring.* Often decisions are made from a selfish perspective. Commit to consider the outcomes and possible hurts that could come from your behavior before acting.
- *Close the chapter.* At some point, it is more beneficial to accept that the past has happened and we've done everything in our power to address past mistakes. It's time to turn the page and accept these events as part of your story. Not all of our story, but a chapter. And, God willing, we have much more life ahead to become better.

They've all contributed to making you who you are. Being grateful for those experiences allows you to move on and truly forgive yourself.

- *Scriptural Support to Break the stronghold of Sin:* Romans 8: 38-39; John 16:33

In the course of our journey through life, we will encounter various C.H.A.I.N.S. that we will have to struggle with. We can overcome these issues and *EMERGE* victorious by engaging in a strategic approach to breaking each of the individual "links." We can move forward by Studying the Word of God and making a commitment to act differently. You must redirect your thoughts toward yourself and show yourself some compassion. This process may require the support of a therapist or coach until you feel strong enough to stand on your own. This won't be easy but it is necessary. God has more waiting for you if you can trust Him to help you break free from the bondage of your C.H.A.I.N.S. You are more than your past mistakes, and you are worth fighting for!!

ANTOINE GARRET

Antoine Garrett's calling is to empower others. Through his writing, speaking, and coaching, he helps individuals and organizations clarify their position, purpose, pursuits and possibilities. Antoine helps others achieve their true potential.

Antoine is the author of the Amazon Best-selling book, **Prepare 4 Takeoff!** *Overcome Beliefs & Behaviors Blocking Your Best Life.* He is also a motivational speaker, and youth minister. Antoine provides powerful and interactive sessions on a variety of topics. Antoine is the host of *Halftime w/ The Coach*- a weekly internet radio show that encourages & empowers listeners to move past obstacles and to focus on the opportunities available to them.

Website:
www.antoinegarrett.com

Break Free From Your C.H.A.I.N.S.

3. EMERGE

YOU ARE A MOUNTAIN!

Thema Azize Serwa

If you are not mindful, you will find yourself overvaluing your wholeness, and despising your brokenness. In order to emerge, whole and healed, you must adequately value both. We live in a world of polarity. Your sanity, your joy, your power is reliant upon your ability to accept both the light and darkness that you are.
The valley is just the bottom of the mountain, and mountains can't stand without valleys. There is not a mountain that exists on the planet today, without a massive collision. Mountains are formed by disasters. Literally, mountains are birthed from the cracking and faulting of the Earth's surface. You don't get the formation of the top of the mountain without some wreckage. The mountain peak is the evidence of what was faulty and broken and it is the most beautiful part of the mountain.

When you learn how to be a mountain, you become the influencer of the weather, the storms, the geography of the planet. Mountains can stand in oceans. Mountains can hold hot lava and erupt destruction or contain the impulse to destroy. Whatever is broken

23

Emerge You Are A Mountain!
and faulty in your life, is being made into something magnificent and holy.

BE THE WISDOM OF THE MOUNTAIN.

What has wrecked in your life? What has pushed you up to higher heights? What has forced you to create healthy boundaries and enforce them?

I remember the day I thought healing my mind, body, and spirit was, what I call, the "divine rebirth". It took the remembrance of suppressed traumas to wake me up. My legacy was on the line. I was told I'd never conceive without help and I was in chronic pain from a reproductive disorder called Polycystic Ovarian Syndrome (PCOS). Out of my darkness, would come light. The odds were stacked against me, I redefined those odds. I healed.

I changed everything in my life: name, income level, career, divorced, reunited in new love, moved, transformed my health, changed my spiritual practice... Finally, I was consistent with waking up at 4 am, cleaning up my home, eating 9-12 servings of cruciferous vegetables, drinking enough water, going to sleep before 10 pm, and meditating an hour per day. I had successfully launched an international business that truly changes lives and it took off. I was aligned with my higher self.

In many ways, I was rebirthed at that time. However, the true emergence that my soul was calling for, was the recognition of who I am, not just what I accomplish. If all you identify as is what you accomplish, God help you the day you fail.

I had a glimpse of myself, but not a complete picture. I was a valley becoming a mountain. There is no true healing without recognition of your God-given self. You cannot heal everything until you love who you recognize.

Thema Azize Serwa

In one of my favorite books, "A Course in Miracles", it says that the greatest miracle one can experience is to see yourself correctly. This implies there is an incorrect way of seeing yourself. Here is the error that is keeping you from emerging into your true self: your deep sense of unworthiness.

Breathe. Feel how you truly feel about your sense of self-worth
.
WHAT CRITERIA ARE YOU USING TO DETERMINE YOUR WORTH?

You will know if you need a greater sense of worthiness by your reactions to events in your life. Your worth is not based upon what you can or cannot do, it is tied to your beingness. The breath of life you are breathing right now has qualified you for a life you enjoy living.

I don't know who it was, when it happened, or why you have believed it for so long but, you are worthy. You are worthy of a self-perception that does not require you to be the cause of what is not working well in your life or in the world. You are worthy to know that you have a God who can do exceedingly, abundantly, more than you have the mental capacity to ask for. I invite you to consider that your birth, is evidence that you are important and worthy.

THE QUESTION YOU NEED TO ASK NOW IS THIS...
ARE THE THINGS, PEOPLE, AND EXPERIENCES IN YOUR LIFE *WORTHY* OF YOU?

I remember the moment this question came to me. I was sitting in my car, holding a court summons for eviction from my home, and with tears running down my face as I pulled up to the home that I feared losing, I screamed and said, "God am I not worthy of this? Am I not good enough for this zip code?" And immediately, I heard a whisper, that said, "Is this home worthy of you?"

25

Emerge You Are A Mountain!
We don't want to face reality until our fantasies fail us. When you are going through hell look for the love in the flames. You think you will be burned, but it truly is simply purification. Honestly, I was not living in my dream home. I was living in something better than what I came from, but it was not what I had on my vision board. I wept as if it was. As if what was happening in that moment was the final chapter for my life. I had some faulty cracks in my foundation, in how I was seeing myself at that moment.

You become a mountain when you not only recognize your God-given self, but also when you radically accept who you see. YOU are your greatest asset. YOU are the missing piece to the puzzle. In you are wells of divine living water. When you truly love yourself, your toleration level, your accessibility, your availability, and your use of your resources change. So, change already.

The best gift you can give yourself is compassion and love when you are looking at the faulty cracks in your foundation. Instead of setting goals to fill those cracks, let's honor them with acceptance. There is no mountain without those cracks.

At times, we use the blessings of God as evidence of our worthiness. I am blessed because I am out of the hood. I am blessed because I have this net worth. I am blessed because I have a certain number of followers on social media. I am blessed because I am married for 20+ years. You were blessed when you were broke. You were blessed when you were eating hot dogs with no buns. You were blessed when no one knew your name. You were blessed when you were single.

GOD DOES NOT NEED YOUR ACCOMPLISHMENTS TO BLESS YOU. SOME OF OUR TRIALS ARE A REMINDER OF THAT.

You do not have to perform for love. Your innate nature is pure, and you are love. The day is coming when you will see the years of overcoming emerge as the peak of your mountain. You will be able

26

to testify about how one rock at a time, you went higher and higher until one-day others could climb you and stand in your strength and glory. You do not need another formula for what to do next in your life, it is time for you to embrace how to simply be. It is time for you to accept yourself deeply, just as you are, in this very moment. Whatever you think is "wrong" with you is not an issue. You are ok.

Some of you reading this will need to abandon your existing value system to be radical with your self-acceptance. Being flawed from the day you left your mother's womb is so deeply embedded in your consciousness that, you believe it. But I offer you this perspective… before you were in the womb, you were *made* in God, fearfully, and wonderfully made. God knew you then before you ever reached Earth. In those intimate moments with God, you learned about this life you are living and made an agreement to come here and live your best life. So, the key to living is being ok with who you are.

ALTHOUGH FORGIVENESS IS NOT REQUIRED, FORGIVE YOURSELF. RELEASE SELF-JUDGMENT AND THE SUBCONSCIOUS NEED TO PUNISH YOURSELF FOR EXISTING.

Imagine how your life will change at the end of this chapter if you truly see yourself as forgiven. Even on your worst day, you are deeply, affectionately, loved and cherished. Forgive yourself for not knowing what you now know. Forgive yourself for mismanagement of your resources. Forgive yourself for the times you did not follow your instincts.

Life is a class. It is natural to learn. Experience is a great teacher. Don't resent what life has taught you. Use the lessons to fortify yourself and see yourself correctly. Another quote from "A Course in Miracles" says, "I will not fear to look within today." You are free to no longer romanticize and give undue credit to your failures. Your identity is one of peace and love.

YOU ARE A MOUNTAIN. EMERGE.

The next time you are near a mountain, ask it, "Are you sorry for being here? Are you angry about what happened last year? How do you feel about the cracks that formed you?" As you stand before that mountain, you will see the power of what you think is wrong with you, and I pray that what you see, gives you the clarity you need to love yourself more deeply. It is that self-love and self-acceptance that will allow you to show up in the word more whole and healed.

THEMA AZIZE SERWA

Thema Azize Serwa is a bestselling author, public speaker, professional coach and educator, and ordained interfaith minister. She is the Empowerment Mogul! She believes that she has served well when you recognize how powerful you are! She is the founder of The Womb Sauna University which offers a world-class certification program for Womb Sauna Practitioners and 24/7 online courses for holistic health education and self-development.

Website:
www.thewombsauna.com

29

Emerge You Are A Mountain!

4. EMERGE

CONFIDENTLY CROWNED:
3 WAYS TO FULLY LAUNCH YOUR CONFIDENCE

LaQuisha Hall

In 2014, I started a business. I mean, you could not tell me anything: I had a business. I named it iEAT when I began: Empower. Aspire. Transform. I believed in my mission of empowering women and girls, being a role model that onlookers could aspire to be like and transforming the minds of all that I encountered through education and direct support. I named my business iEAT because I am naturally thin and I was tired of being asked the question, "Do you eat?" I believed that my *work* should speak for me: Not only did I eat in real life, but I ate so much that I was able to regurgitate it back into others and create "full" community leaders. However, this double entendre came back to bite me instead of me taking a bite of it…

I began to be contacted by potential customers and I was asked, "What type of cooking do you do?" or "Where did you gain your culinary skills?" The truth is that I don't cook at all. Not even in real life. I recognized about a year later that I had inappropriately named my business. The rebranding process had to transpire.

31

Confidently Crowned

I considered what my strengths were, what my focuses were and how I lived my life every day. I knew without a shadow of a doubt that I was strong when it came to empowering others or making them feel confident and royal. I focused on uplifting others but I did it in my own way. For example, every young lady or woman who has ever met me has been referred to as a queen and gently reminded of why they deserved this title. I lived my life as a queen but didn't realize it until someone else explained my worth to me.

I also love, absolutely adore, fashion! I always get a thrill from dressing up and looking my best. As a result, I began life as a fashion blogger in 2012. Corner Curl Girl was born to inspire others on how to style clothing they already had in their closet and to give other natural hair beauties ideas on how to style their hair.

I discovered a reoccurring thread in both aspects of my life: I gave others confidence.

But, I did not educate others on how to be confident through the traditional means: I did it in the most queenly, unique way I knew how… in my own way. In the fashion world, this would be a couture way because there is no other garment made like the one you see on the runway, nor would one be made like it. No one else empowers the way that I do. I don't just call others queens, I have lived the life, literally and figuratively.

Hence, Couture'd Confidence was born on January 1st, 2015.

While appropriately naming my business was one of the biggest lessons I learned, there were 3 additional important lessons that I want to share with you. There are many ways you can build your confidence. *Here are three things I personally did to strengthen my confidence:*

1. Create an authentic goal.
2. Find purpose in your pain.
3. Work because it is necessary.

But you are a chosen people, a royal priesthood, a holy nation,
God's special possession, that you may declare the praises of him
who called you out of darkness into his wonderful light. 1 Peter 2:9

CREATE AN AUTHENTIC GOAL

Authenticity is all about the perception of the credibility of your goal. It relates to the ability to accomplish the envisioned experiences and creating a reliable solution to the problem it seeks to solve.

In creating an authentic goal, you must:

- TELL TRUE STORIES

I have successfully overcome low self-esteem due to being naturally thin and survived witnessing domestic violence as a child, as well as being a victim of incest. Whenever I give a presentation, no matter the topic, I share these true stories. Often, many of the audience members connect with what I share and are amazed at my confidence. In sharing my truth, I have gained the trust of my audience and drew closer to my goal of becoming a distinguished speaker and budding artist. Create stories that are relatable and help others reach their goals.

- DECIDE ON THE ELEMENTS OF YOUR GOAL

Tone: The tone is the voice of the goal. It is what makes the goal recognizable, distinctive, and unique. Every time I meet a young lady or a woman, I refer to her as "Queen". Now, whenever someone meets me not only do they feel comfortable sharing their stories with me but they also refer to me as "Queen" as well.

Design: Design includes elements that are used to identify the goal.

Whenever you see me or anything that represents me, you will see the colors purple, teal, and gold. These colors were purposefully chosen. Purple is the awareness color for domestic violence prevention, teal is the awareness color for sexual abuse prevention and gold is the color I used to remind the audiences I empower that they were not born to walk on concrete, they were born to walk on gold (they are not to remain in the same place their entire lives but rather elevate). If I were to be associated with a symbol, it would definitely be a crown. I am also known for my slogan, #theUnbotheredQueen, because I have successfully obtained too many big achievements and victories to be worried about small obstacles.

- SELF-PROMOTE SHAMELESSLY

If you follow me on any social media, you will be updated on my speaking engagements, awards received, events held and even my latest fashionable ensemble. It is important that you share your goal aggressively. Let everyone know that you do a certain activity and the way you do it. You will be held accountable for your goal by onlookers.

Many are the plans in a person's heart, but it is the LORD's purpose that prevails. Proverbs 19:21

FIND PURPOSE IN YOUR PAIN

There are two main types of people on the planet. There are those who continue hurting long after the challenge has gone and there are those who find new inspiration in their problems. I am the latter.

All have a story to which they became established. The story becomes the inspiration for moving the vision of the goal you want to accomplish. There are people who are survivors, similar to me, that had problems with being confident because some person, group or situation attempted to snatch it from them in their past. Or you may have had trouble getting a nanny when you gave birth and you started a nanny service. Others lost their jobs and decided to turn their hobbies into a business.

If you are seeking your purpose, you must sort through the pain that you suffered. The purpose will be strong enough to propel you in both thick and thin because you overcame the pain. You must also be able to live the purpose regardless of the condition of your lifestyle. This creates the passion and gives you the energy to push you through the great and not so great times.

The best way to identify your purpose is to look at conditions that got you into the problem. What solutions can prevent any other person from falling into the same trap? Look at the lessons you have learned from the pain. How will your purpose effectively and positively impact others?

"For I know the plans I have for you," declares the LORD, "plans to prosper you and not to harm you, plans to give you hope and a future. Jeremiah 29:11

WORK BECAUSE IT IS NECESSARY

I spent about 5 years serving in the community as a volunteer. I did not always get paid to share my story, help a hurting woman or present an engaging workshop to youth. I did it for free because I was so passionate about helping others that cost did not matter to me. I went to every women's shelter, abuse prevention event, women's empowerment session that I could. I learned from observation and by being hands on the amount of work involved in pulling others out of the situations that I used to be in. Now, of course, as an expert, I am deserving of the compensation of my time spent gaining and imparting my knowledge, but I truly believe that I would not be where I am today without having to freely engage first. Because I spent so much time "freely serving" it was not hard for me to transition into proving that I am not only authentic, but I am a hard worker deserving to be heard.

MOVE OUT THERE

I was in constant contact with community leaders that I volunteered for, seeking opportunities to elevate. One of my experiences was being a volunteer for local women's empowerment organization for 10 years. I watched from behind the scenes how to plan events that leave audiences in tears, witnessed the founders make personal investments to enlarge their territory and watch their brand grow. I traveled locally and abroad to hold up the banner of sisterhood. I dreamed that one day I could be a coach, a speaker, a facilitator, a mentor, a woman who could heal a woman to heal a nation. I desired so much to speak on a "main stage" and in April 2016, I was able to actualize this dream. To see my face in the program book and stand on a profound platform with some of the most powerful women I had ever met empowered me in so many ways. My heart still leaps when I think of all that I faced individually and as a part of a team. At the end of the day, the volunteering, the sisterhood, the authenticity became real.

VOLUNTEER IN YOUR COMMUNITY

There are many ways that a purpose-driven person can assist the community around them. You could start a free youth mentorship program, community support program, city cleaning, or a workshop with the target market. Volunteering makes the community feel that they are a part of what you establish. With this mindset, the community can embrace your message with ease. Building a community is not an event but a process that takes time. There is no silver (or golden) bullet to building—you have to blend a number of strategies to create strength. Moreover, you need to have a method of measuring the results of your efforts and making adjustments where necessary. The process of building takes the entire lifetime of your purpose.

I define confidence. I am the Unbothered Queen, walking on gold to fulfill my purpose. Join me in this confidence journey!

And we know that in all things God works for the good of those who love him, who have been called according to his purpose.
Romans 8:28

LAQUISHA HALL

LaQuisha Hall is an award-winning philanthropist, inspirational speaker and author who empowers her community through mentoring girls, uplifting abuse survivors and blogging about looking and feeling great while living life on purpose? LaQuisha Hall, the "Unbothered Queen" of Confidence, goes far beyond what is expected of her. There was a time in LaQuisha's life where she was not confident in much. She struggled through low self-esteem due to being naturally thin, witnessed domestic violence as a child and was sexually abused by clergy as a teen. Now an international advocate for herself and others, LaQuisha actively works to empower women and youth to overcome catastrophe through Couture'd Confidence. Her "walk on gold" philosophy teaches communities to step off of familiar territory to do extraordinary things. LaQuisha has empowered others to empower others for over a decade and has no plans of stopping!

Website:
www.laquishahall.com

5. EMERGE

DON'T BELIEVE THE HYPE! YOU ARE CREATIVE

Rock Mitchell

As far as my memory serves me, I've always been a creative person. From singing in the choir and playing musical instruments in church as a young boy, to my love for watching a good movie with my mom, dad and older brother on Friday night. Remember TGIF on ABC on Friday nights? Those were the good old days! I would imagine that's when my imagination and creative flare started to really take shape. However, I can't say that it was all me. My mother along with the rest of her side of the family are all creatives. All of them singing and playing, acting, painting and the like. I have Ford blood running through my veins for sure. My Dad, on the other hand, was "straight to the business" and "relationship building "kind of guy. I had the best of both worlds, growing up with a skilled creative and a guy that knew how to spec out the job and get the project done while leading the team to victory. Might I say, if you are going to win in business or any other aspiration, you have to have a bit of all three, creativity, business acumen and interpersonal skills.

Don't Believe the Hype! You Are Creative

Let's jump right into it and not waste any time. When it comes to creativity some believe either you have it or you don't. Don't believe that lie! Everyone has a bit of creativity. The problem is, some are so close to a thing that innovation does not have room to breathe let alone add value. Google defines creativity as the use of the imagination or original ideas, especially in the production of artistic work. You are a masterpiece made in God's own image. God, being the perfectionist that he is, knew what he wanted to convey when He made you the way he did. Somehow, we've lost some of our God ability (the ability to create) when we think about our stuff. I'm pretty sure crafting your life falls into the category of creative work. As we've been discussing in this book, you are called to be the CEO of your life. Using your imagination to breathe life into ideas, goals, and visions you have makes you creative!

People often pay someone like me thousands of dollars in project and retainer fees to come up with clever ideas and to execute them all while you run off to do the big important business stuff. Well, if that is you or you would approach it similarly if you had the chance, your thinking may be all wrong.

You're telling me you had enough creative power to think of great money-making ideas, causes to bring people together, music or something else meaningful, but then when it comes to shaping the brand and marketing, you run off because that's not your thing? Well, here is a word to the wise, you better make it your thing, quick. The world has already shifted to media and the creative realm. Not being able to execute creatively is going to be what kills businesses in the twenty-first century. Don't let that be you! Whether it is a business or your life that you are running as a CEO, tap into and fully harness your creative power.

Where do most creatives start? They start with inspiration. Not every creative project or masterpiece began in the mind of the creative. Be honest with the fact that at times you need a good jump start to bring your ideas to life. Sometimes you don't know what you like or want until you see it. I start with a lot of projects with atmosphere, yep, atmosphere. To get in the right creative vein, my physical space has to be conducive to what I need to create. I love to work from my home, but sometimes the area is just not right. Starbucks or my office at work offer the décor needed to bring inspiration. Not to mention as a child my favorite place in the whole world was IKEA, I often go there to walk around and feel the vibe.

Another great way to jump-start your creative flow is to immerse yourself in color pallets and music. I find that innovation begins to flow when you find tones and visuals that spark inspiration. Don't forget to research other creative works that are similar in nature to what you look to accomplish. Be it video, graphics, photography, written or audible copy, it never hurts to let someone else do the hard work first. Recreating the wheel is the biggest waste of time.

Do it your way! As you start or continue your creative journey, you are not going to always have the technical know-how to accomplish your goal. Truthfully you may not even know anyone who can achieve the desired result. Here is where innovation comes in. When I first started making visuals, I had no clue on how to recreate the things I saw in movies or tv. It took trial and error for me to learn that my desired outcome was just a few more tries away. I learned how to get what I wanted out of the equipment that I could afford. I was a part of the DSLR revolution.

What's the DSLR revolution? It was the time back in the early 2000s when camera makers started putting video functions in their photography cameras. What's so significant about that you ask? Weren't there already camcorders? Well, to keep it simple, it was the functionality of being able to completely control the functions of the video (like a cinema camera) that made small budget creators eager to jump at the opportunity to see what they could do with a camera that looked like a big budget film camera for just under a few thousand dollars.

I tried my hand at it. I bought a Canon T2i and switched it to video mode. I started recording everything. At that time Apple came out

41

Don't Believe the Hype! You Are Creative
with iMovie, an inexpensive way to throw your clips together, add a title and music and export your project. iMovie was perfect for me. I would record tons of stuff and spend hours cutting it together to show friends and family. When I felt it was good enough, I would even put it on Myspace and or Facebook.

That leads to my next point; IT DOESN'T HAPPEN OVERNIGHT. Getting good takes time. It takes time to develop the necessary skills to produce at a high level. The learning curve is very steep. Be it copy, graphic design, audio recording or film production, there is a lot one must learn, but that's ok. The process of learning the technicalities of creativity is what introduces you to error. Not just error in yourself, but it helps you to gauge where the competition is. I found that by observing others, you can determine where your deficiencies are. I would often look at a film produced by others and think "there's something wonky about this footage." The ordinary viewer could not see it, but because of trial and error, study and research I could see that this person shot a slow-motion video in the wrong frame rate and tried to slow it down in post (editing) without enough frames to make the image smooth and buttery. This type of thing was the perfect reminder of what not to do when I went to work on my next project.

These next few paragraphs are for my creatives that want to build a business doing what they love. Bear with me for just a moment while I drop a jewel. For some odd reason, the general public thinks that creating something out of nothing should not cost as much as it does. Can I tell you, being creative can be lucrative, only if you value yourself correctly and market to the right set of customers Most creatives have a hard time setting their price, and I get it. It's a matter of self-awareness. Some are just starting and don't want to overvalue their current skill set or they lower their price point based on whether they think the client can afford it. Nope, all wrong! There are tiers to this industry like any other. An NBA rookie is not getting the same contract as LeBron James. A rookie creative spends much time giving away his or her craft for free promotion and public facing practice.

It's hard to know when to transition from practice to professional, from free to paid and paid to really paid. Well here's how I gauge the transition. Practice is when you're unsure of your exact workflow and how you're going to complete the project from beginning to end. Because the client is taking a risk on you, there's no reason to charge them money while you try to figure out what you're doing. Paid is when you've figured out your workflow and know what equipment you need, the time the job will take, and the other resources needed to produce the project. Really paid is when you have a catalog of clients that are excited to work with you and are your chief marketers. Really paid is when you've invested in your own business.

I remember a few years back, I knew it was time to take my skill set to the next level, so I bought the tools needed to do that. When I pulled the trigger and bought a $6,000 camera, I knew I was getting there. Now my clients were responsible for paying for that, and I could not cheapen myself just for an opportunity anymore. Needless to say, I bought that camera in January, it paid for itself by March. Now that's pro if you ask me.

Ok, now I'm back from talking to my creative business folks. Interpersonal skills are a must when it comes to being a great creative or even being a business owner with an artistic flare. It's more profound than just being able to create, it's the ability to have vision enough to see what goes where and when. These days I'm known more of as a producer and creative director than a videographer. Why? That's the way I want to be seen. I've spent a good portion of my life in corporate culture learning the art of relationships and business all the while lending ideas and my flair for aesthetic.

Now that my primary source of income is being creative, I find myself more on the executive end of the project giving direction, producing, at times even financing projects. Don't get me wrong, I still do the shooting and editing, but I spend far more time in meetings with clients crafting out ideas, writing proposals (thanks to C. Simon) traveling and taking late night calls to sure up a deal that's made a turn in a different direction. I love what I do. To be successful in this new creative space takes lots of humility and an excellent choice in words.

An excellent creative has learned the art of articulating the vision of someone else who does not have the words or ability to make it come to life. A prime example of this is when you go to a tattoo artist with an idea. Once you give the artist the idea, they make time to mock up their interpretation of what you've expressed. Typically, when you've returned, they have captured exactly what you saw in your mind. That's an excellent creative, someone who can take their ideas or someone else's and make them a reality.

Start today! Whether you're already a creative person or feel as though you don't have a drop of creativity in you, do something. It will make your life and or business all the more rewarding. God has made you in his image. Since he had the power to create, you have the power to create. What will life be like when you tap into and harness that power?

ROCK MITCHELL

Rock Mitchell, a multifaceted professional living in Towson Maryland is committed to providing creative insight to a wide spectrum of brands, non-profits and corporate entities. Through creative direction, execution and production Rock has help to increase sales, participation and brand awareness across many industries. Rock is committed to change locally and internationally through his work in Baltimore with non-profit and faith based organizations and work in Africa providing fresh water to remote villages and funding schooling need schools in Ghana. Currently, Rock heads marketing for one of Maryland's premier mental health organizations and is making a significant impact in changing the culture and stigmas surrounding mental health services.

Follow him @rockmitchell

Don't Believe the Hype! You Are Creative

6. EMERGE

IN YOUR HEALTH

Taryn Mitchell

I'd like to start by saying that I do not claim to be a weight loss expert, I am just your everyday mom who was able to lose a total of 86 pounds all natural. To date, I am maintaining and still losing weight by simply changing my lifestyle. I made simple changes to my diet, increased my workout activity, and most importantly changed my mindset. I am a certified Personal Trainer and a certified Cranked Up Cardio instructor. I am currently working to earn my NASM certifications in nutrition and group fitness.

The backdrop for my experience has been growing up in the United States and living during a time when convenience drives everything. A time when everyone wants everything quick fast and in a hurry. I begin to think back to 2006 when I got married. I weighed 170 pounds and my husband was about 205 pounds. At that time, we were considered to be overweight, even though we didn't look or feel heavy. Over the years we continued to eat fast food, have children, and sometimes we were just plain lazy. During that time frame, I gained about seventy-two pounds and my husband gained about eighty pounds.

Thinking back, it was like we were a part of a medical experiment trying to determine who can gain the most weight. During our second year of marriage; we ate fast food and or takeout every day for an entire year. Yes 365 days of breakfast, lunch, and dinner were take-out. Whether it was going out to eat at a restaurant or calling to place a to-go order, it was always take out. We ate late at night and many times went straight to sleep. It seemed as though we were always on the go and eating out was simply convenient and easy. Even after having children we continued to eat out occasionally.

Like most people, we have started and stopped many times trying to achieve weight loss and working to be healthier. But we just could not seem to stick with it. There are thousands of weight loss books, manuals, videos, and methods and being honest we have tried quite a few of them. What makes this short chapter different from everything else is that it's written by a married woman who works a full-time job, raises two little boys, runs a small business, and is currently a full-time student. According to my schedule, I should have no time to focus on losing weight. With all of these barriers to healthy living, it really came down to a decision. I had to make a decision once and for all. Would I continue down this path of destruction until my body gives out or would I choose to live?

This chapter will detail the core concepts that I used during my weight loss and healthy living journey. Again, by no means do I imply that I am a professional weight loss expert, but like many other efforts in life sometimes you just need help getting started. Your goal may not be weight loss. Perhaps you just desire to eat healthier, exercise more or take better care of your body. The principles that I am about to share will assist you with any of these goals.

The key to living a successful life is having the right attitude and mindset. Change starts with how you think. If you think defeated, you have already lost the battle. I know healthy living is challenging, but it is obtainable and so worth it. Use this to jumpstart your new journey to living a healthier life and loving the only body you have been gifted.

I used these five core concepts to assist me with my goal.
1. Choice
2. Determination
3. Focus
4. Commitment
5. Faith

CORE CONCEPTS

CHOICE: Mentally making a decision, judging the merits of multiple options and selecting one of those options.

You are in control of your life. As adults, we decide every day what time we will get up, what we will wear, where we will live, and what we will eat. You are the "commander" of your body, it's up to you to fuel it properly for your daily journey. One day I decided to take make healthier lifestyle choices. I got tired of feeling tired. I got tired of secretly despising how I looked and felt. I hated shopping, nothing in the store would fit me. I didn't want to walk to the park with my children in the spring or summer, it was too hot, and I hated to sweat. I didn't find myself attractive with my clothes off and it affected my intimate relationship with my husband. He loved me at any size, but as a woman, if we don't feel sexy it affects how we respond to our mates. I was full of confidence in front of people but, secretly I dreaded getting dressed. On September 8, 2014, I finally made the choice to do something about my weight. I decided that I was worth sacrificing a few nights on the couch, a few slices of pizza, a few cups of soda, to reach my ultimate goal of being healthy.

Choice has to outweigh your feelings! The choice you make today about your health has to drive you to the finish line. When you make a choice to live a healthier life everything that you do from that day forth should help you towards that choice you made. In simple, YOU have to make the choice no one can make that choice for you.

DETERMINATION: A positive emotion that involves persevering towards a difficult goal in spite of obstacles.

Determination occurs prior to you reaching your goal and should motivate behaviors that will help you achieve your goal. Thinking positive and speaking positively on your road to better health is very important. Positive emotions drive you towards positive results. Determination pushed me to lose 86 pounds in 10 months. Every day was not perfect, but every day was an opportunity for me to make strides towards my ultimate goal. Every morning I woke up before my alarm and looked myself in the mirror and said, "Girl, you can, and you will succeed." I did that for one month and in that one month, I lost 17 pounds. I attribute much of my success during this journey to speaking positively. When I felt like quitting, I would yell, "Let's Get It!" I would be on the treadmill crying but, I never quit. I was determined that this time things would be different. You have to go from the state of desiring to be healthy to the state of being determined to be healthy.

When you desire something, it's more like a dream or a wish that can dissolve. A true want is a hunger inside of you that never dies. Your current level of results is nothing more than a residual outcome of your past thoughts, feelings, and actions. This has nothing to do with what you are capable of doing unless you continue to make the same choices. Think about your results as a mirror. A mirror doesn't judge, it doesn't say something is good or bad, right or wrong. It doesn't edit or delete a mirror just reflects back whatever is in front of it. If you look in the mirror and you are not pleased with your results, you have to be determined to change your methods to get the results you want. It takes time and patience. We must learn to trust the process.

FOCUS: To concentrate on a particular person, place, or thing until you can see it clearly.

Focus is a required step needed to obtain long lasting & life-changing health. Set goals and write out a tangible plan then everyday work towards those goals. During my weight loss process, I learned that focusing on my ultimate and immediate goals helped me to stay focused. I did not focus on what I could not and did not want to do. Instead, focus on the positives & you will succeed. Every day will not be easy but every stride that you make towards your goals will push you closer to living a healthier life. I learned to focus my attention on the change and not the results. Sometimes you will feel that your work is in vain because the results are not coming as fast as you would like to see. This only can discourage you from pushing forward; I decided to focus on meal prepping, focus on being more active, focus on trying new things, focus on drinking more water, and focus less on how my body was changing.

Focusing on the change helped me to develop new eating habits and new workout habits. Those new habits are what changed my life; I knew I was tired of dieting and trying to lose weight fast. I was fed up with focusing on quick weight loss and only led me to disappointment and depression. I would lose ten pounds and gain it back, I never address the real issue using those quick products. Those products did not make me focus, they did not make me use will power or determination. Losing weight my way required me to think and be more self-aware of what I was consuming. Focus on changing your habits and your new habits will change you.

COMMITMENT: Dedicated to a cause, loyal to something, the attitude of working hard to accomplish something.

I know you are wondering what commitment has to do with living a healthier lifestyle. Commitment is a monumental component of successful completion of a goal. Most people think about relationships between people when they hear the word commitment, but I have learned that the relationship that we have with ourselves is often neglected. We commit to other people, things, and even places but never commit to ourselves leaving us sometimes empty and drained. During my weight loss journey, I discovered that I never truly committed to myself, I just merely existed. I focused all of my attention on my husband, ministry, my children, work, and helping other people; those commitments held a greater weight in my life than the commitment to Taryn. After becoming frustrated with myself, I did a self-evaluation and made some adjustments. I committed to loving me first then everything else follows behind.

This journey to health can be frustrating but just like in relationships, you don't leave because you are frustrated. You take time to adjust, determine the cause of the frustration, and work towards making things better. It's the same process when you are working to lose weight. Committing to this journey means that you understand there will be valleys, mountain tops, mow hills, ditches, rocks, mud, and more but you will refuse to quit. I can remember my weight stall for about 3 months the scale kept going up and down up and down; the old me wanted to give up but the committed me understood the purpose of the process. Commitment kept me going when the motivation faded, commitment pushed me to get up a 5 am, commitment pushed me to eat the same meals every day, commitment pushed me to drink plenty of water, commitment drove me to obtain the results I desired. Ask yourself, am I committed or am I just motivated?

FAITH: Strong belief in something or someone, belief in God, confidence in God. Hope in something that you cannot see.

My weight loss story was birthed through my faith. I can remember trying on many different occasions to lose weight and I would always throw in the towel before I reached my goal. In September 2014 something was different, I decided to pray about my weight loss and eating habits. I was on the treadmill at the gym barely walking and my face was filled with tears as the people beside me were running sprints on the treadmills next to me. I began to weep and pray, I asked God, "Why can't I lose weight? His response to me was so clear, "I gave you the power, now what are you going to do with it?" I was in such awe that I dried my tears and I picked up the speed just a little on my treadmill. I think I did 30 minutes that day. From that day forth I have never looked back. It has not been perfect, and I have had my moments, but I refused to go back to my old way of thinking. I decided to actually use my power.

In life, we often times apply our faith to material things or life situations, but never to our physical selves unless we are sick. You must believe in yourself. While praying that day, God reminded me that I was fearfully and wonderfully made and that He equipped me with the power to do anything that I put my mind to. That encounter with God changed my whole outlook on life. It made me realized that I was hindering myself from growing because of fear. I feared failure. I feared the reaction of other people. I feared letting myself down. I feared the unknown. Maybe you find yourself in this very place of fear and it is paralyzing you from moving forward. Today, I declare that you are free. You are free to get your life back. You are free to push forward. I encourage you to write down your weight loss and healthy lifestyle goals today. Pray over those goals, recite those goals, and work towards those goals daily. Your faith will be the bridge to get you through this journey when things get tough. The journey will not be easy, but it will be worth it. I encourage you to keep a journal documenting your journey.

TARYN MITCHELL

My name is Taryn Mitchell. I was born and raised in Baltimore. I am a mom, wife, certified personal trainer, fitness coach, author, and a motivational speaker.

After getting married, having children, experiencing real happiness, and stability, I became severely overweight and suffered from self-esteem issues. About four years ago I finally came to the realization that I owed my children more, I owed myself more. I made a change, a 90lb. change. Once the commitment to my change was cemented, I began to help other women like me to realize that change was within reach. Within the last four years well over 1800 women from across the country have taken my lead/coaching and dropped a range of five to 57 lbs. I coach these women virtually and locally by empowering them to know their worth. I never imagined that my personal struggle with self-esteem and obesity would lead me to where I am today. I currently host online weight loss challenges, that are very successful and I am in the process of completing my second book "The Transformation".

Website:
www.coachtaryn.com

7. Emerge
in your wellness: The Brand of You

Tony Triumph

The art of building an intricate, world-class brand, recognized and respected by the masses is a boundless art. Father, please help us along this journey to fortifying our brilliance, for we truly know not what we've gotten ourselves into.

Honestly, I had no idea what I'd plummeted myself into until the dust began settling a few years ago.

My journey launched when I moved to New York City with $350 in my pocket, and the majority of my belongings stuffed into the back of my 98' Volkswagen Passat. Reluctantly, I was an aspiring fashion model that was fed up with life in Maryland, and plagued by insufficient hope towards my dream of success. I'd pondered through these wishes and dreams my entire childhood, so quite frankly I couldn't hold back any longer. It was a freezing February night, smack in the winter of 2007. As cold as the weather veered, my drive was what kept me warm. It was as if someone had lit a fire beneath my feet. Unbeknownst to me, my friends thought I was crazy, my mother was worried yet prayerful, and I remember one of my aunts said, "but why are you just letting this whole modeling thing take over your life?" Even with me having achieved the status of becoming a full-time model over the first few years of my adult life, the journey wasn't actually about becoming a model. A revelation that didn't strike me until about 5 years in. That my pursuit of modeling was only the necessary bait needed to jumpstart the journey.

Low and behold, these were the beginning incubators that would later connect me to the encore of my career. My first taste of God's many disruptions (often times leaving me angry from disappointment) that led me down the road towards my greater good. Powered by faith and resilience to overcome my own self-doubts, to the plaques of a poor quality of life and the often immoral distractions of non-stop partying. Temptations conveniently available while mustering through life in a big city, and pursuing a career in Arts & Entertainment.

New York City would become the place to master my craft, unleash opportunities and conquer what I felt were inadequacies; fears that were magnified by the toxic expectations and crippling limitations of growing up in Baltimore.

Building an entrepreneurial enterprise, amongst becoming an editor, and eventually, a Journalist, while working with people and businesses to build phenomenal products, was next on my life goals list after modeling. Without knowing where to start or how to fully nurture this next chapter, I began traveling extensively. From a brief stint in Los Angeles, then off to live in London, followed by life Paris. Tackling multiple markets, I soon learned that these experiences, and new titles to my career, in addition to building the knowledge, skills, and network needed to nurture the vision, I was ultimately building the multi-faceted personal brand that I had envisioned from my childhood. I was checking off every career box one by one, and the life I'd wished, dreamed and prayed for was growing right before my eyes. The only catch- these goals were not manifesting in the ways I had expected them to. At this point my mother was proud (but still wanted me to get a 'real job'), my friends and family were motivated by my success, and my pastor, Dr. Karen Bethea, kept repeating "You have truly defied the odds."

As the journey continued, I began thanking God for the faith, drive and agility I didn't even realize I had. People ask me all the time, "Is there anything about your journey you would change?" As far as the life lessons go: no. Would I have liked to have been better prepared, handle certain situations with more grace and come out this process with fewer battle scars? Absolutely. What I most recently integrated into my journey is initiative I call 'wellness within the win.'

Wellness, which I'll start off saying, begins with the bravery to commit to the process of the vision. Releasing thoughts of guilt from the very start. Planning ahead while leveraging an extraordinary goal with plenty of excitement. Not consuming nonsense throughout the journey, and nurturing myself through and into environments that resemble the life that I'm building.

Feeling rushed and consumed, but acting on the opposite. In this current era of quickness and instant-access, I will instead relax and rejuvenate when society's expectations taunt me. I pledge to produce more of what's true to my life goals and push forward long withheld projects and ideas. I pledge not to overwork myself or add too much to my plate. My life will operate at a pace that is nourishing to my well-being and keeps me full of energy and humility.

My goal is to make available the same sensible knowledge and insight to my tribe of go-getters that could've saved me a ton of hardship throughout this process of building my dreams.

As I continue to fulfill the next chapters of my journey, I'll leave you with a few of my special gems to conquer your own goals, and seize faith in the Lord's ability to manifest them.

STAY CONNECTED TO YOUR ROOTS

Often times we get so excited about our new journey and tired with the backlash from our family and friends that we disconnect from them. I'll urge you to be patient, and stay connected. Their fear is just as much a part of your journey as their support. Sometimes we get so sucked into the vortex of chasing success that we forget how much we need our loved ones to keep us grounded and on track. We are still living in our earthly bodies, therefore God will often rely on those closest to us to keep us aligned with His guidance, His will, and His protection. The only people you should be disconnecting from are the naysayers and haters. And even those, you keep a watchful eye on to remind yourself of how far you've come and how blessed you are! Keep close the words of love and support from those kind-hearted people within your community, network, and family who've supported you from day one. Write down their words of encouragement in a journal, or type them up and print them out. When building your brand, dark days are part of the journey. Your roots keep you powered by faith, connected to humility and steady on your most rightful path. The most abundant thing in our lives that we take for granted is to be surrounded by family and friends that truly love us. Unconditionally, it is one of the deepest foundations to your power.

SOOTHE YOUR SOUL

Ordered steps and crucial life decisions come from the sacred place of soul soothing. Do not neglect your guiding light from within. Turn-up your light and beam it on the world like a flashlight. Taking pride in who you really are, and what you truly want out of life. There is nothing along your journey that can dampen or darken your brand with this inner light.

"All days of the afflicted are evil, but he who is of a merry heart has a continual feast." Proverbs 15:15

Keyword: feast. Feast equals to your prize, your happiness, and your abundance coming from a happy heart. A happy heart brings inspiration, love, joy, and peace which are prerequisites to being able to handle the Brand of You that you're walking into. Soothing the soul equals pure-hearted and purpose-driven daily actions, which instantaneously leaves limited space for disorder within your life. Soothing out anything that makes the soul cry and takes your mind out of focus. Draw close to anything that reminds you of a good time in your life where you were whole; focused, happy, financially stable, beautiful, well-fed, well-rested, loved, and glowing. Go back to that place and protect it. Lead the soothing of your soul through thoughts of peace and beauty.

REDEEM YOURSELF

At some point within your journey, you'll get so absorbed by the dynamics 'making it' that it'll feel as if you're losing yourself. Things will pick-up at such a fast rate, all within a vortex you've never felt or experienced before. You'll be forced to step back, assess, and face the downtime needed to process the remnants of your daily functions and interactions. All of this, just in order to analyze the next steps of your journey.

I call it the conquest of the spirit. The redemption of the soul. Revealing all that you've experienced, and redeeming all that's needed to continue the journey. A balancing period within the process, that which builds your lifestyle and mindset to match the Brand of You that's currently under construction. Taking time to savor life's moments that elevate your energy and push you forward. Recognizing the battles that come with new territory, and conquer them in ways that are contrary to who you are, but teach you to be adaptable and harness new skills for the next dimension! To enter your next phases with grace and preparedness in ways that break your comfort zone, but don't break your spirit. This is the part of the

The Brand of You
journey where you recognize the hard work paying off, but need reminders like Isaiah 54:17, *"No weapon formed against thee shall prosper[...]"*

RELEASE AND YOU WILL MULTIPLY

Let go of everything that does not serve you. Every level of involvement that pushes you back, nails you down, creates dread and suffocates you with self-doubt. This is your inner being telling you to flee. Keep releasing people and habits to create space for bigger and better. Get comfortable with shifts in order to maximize the coming level of success.

Release and roar towards glorious settings, happy people, and good doers. If crops and trees grow in the light, and you come from the same ethereal source, why would you not bask and multiply in the same way? Can crops grow with burdens and the weight of bricks holding them down? We know that roses grew from concrete, but wouldn't you rather an entire bouquet? Release layers from your life and never be afraid to leave things behind. To cut back and declutter and embrace the mindset that less is more. Holding onto to old stuff that no longer has value requires expensive maintenance, and will eventually turn into a liability. Imagine incorporating this into people, products, and processes in your life that no longer have value, or have run their course.

A simple prayer: "Lord, help me to decrease in my flesh, so that you may increase in your will."

Wishing you a journey of great revelation, Godly vision, and favor.

TONY TRIUMPH

Tony Triumph is a Brand Strategist, Writer, Editor and Entrepreneur who has become interculturally recognized for his expertise in fashion, lifestyle, and CPG brand development consultancy. A native of 'Charm City', Baltimore, MD, Tony is currently living in New York City, but consistently travels to both local and international markets for assignments.

Tony is the CEO of The Triumphant Group, a New York City based Product & Brand Management firm which oversees the strategic growth, development and awareness of today's most thriving brands. As Editor and Founder, Tony also manages growth and development of the fast growing digital platform, The Triumphant Scoop. His past collaborations include: Barney's New York, PUMA, Ben Sherman, Intelligent Nutrients, SONY, Wix.com, Cadillac, and Hyatt Hotels. Tony has been featured in The Huffington Post, Essence, EBONY, Complex, and The Washington Post.

Website:
www.triumphantscoop.com

The Brand of You

8. EMERGE
CLOAKED FOR THE PURSUIT & STYLED FOR PURPOSE

Justin Shaw

"When I see you, I see God's Glory." My eyes began to flood with tears as those words parted my client's lips. We were sitting at a tall wooden table, eating dinner while I designed his new custom shirts.

Those words pierced my soul because he had witnessed where I used to be, but now he could see the testimony of where God had brought me through my obedience. All I had was a vision to produce quality garments for purpose-driven gentleman. I wanted to ensure they were polished, presentable and prepared to produce impact.

As an adolescent, I lacked the ability to find value in my own voice. I would simply refrain from expressing my input about any topic because I lacked either the posture, charisma, or the background to speak on such things. My comments? Irrelevant. My presence? Hidden. My impact? Minimal.

Cloaked for The Pursuit

But then I found a space of free expression. Clothing. I began sporting suits from Macy's, H&M, and Forever 21. I received a few compliments daily from others. Then I started to develop confidence from these consistent positive words of affirmation. These words began to etch their way into my psyche.

Time prolonged and I began to notice that my outer image would set the tone for those around me. That's when I decided that there was an opportunity to produce impact through apparel. I launched my company, Shaw's Covenant Custom Clothier, to shift environments of the end user of my products.

Because of this God-given assignment, I have been able to produce hundreds of custom garments nationwide for men pursuing their purpose. I see clients daily developing into something greater, just because they are sporting their custom garments.

What do you cloak yourself in daily? Do you realize that your image reflects your attitude and actions towards the pursuit? Do you simply wake up and toss on garments quickly with no thought of what you pieced together? Perhaps you do take the time each day to prepare your attire. Nonetheless, this plays a significant role in your mindset & influence. Imagine if a soldier was lackadaisical on grabbing the proper equipment before he ventures out for war. He tossed his fatigue jacket on but forgets to put on his bulletproof vest. A sniper forgets to toss on a ghillie suit to blend in with his environment, so he's stuck wearing his standard uniform. This would critically alter their success in combat because they are not properly clothed for the environment.

It is unfortunate but it is a reality that the world judges you off simple stereotypes and how you present yourself. Which is why your dress is more important than most realize. If you are wearing the cleanest suit or sleekest dress with red bottoms, people will classify you as wealthy. This is one of the many imperfections we have in the world, but it's implanted in our subconscious mind. We are trained from a young age through television, reading, social media, or even through personal experience these visual stereotypes. This is one of the reasons you should maximize your appearance. I'm not saying to do this to persuade others to believe your wealthy, but to grant you access to people. It may provide you their discernment, curiosity, or leniency.

I can recall on several occasions when I was driving on the beltway going 25 mph above the speed limit and I would get pulled over. Every time the officer came to the car, he wasn't nervous and would let me go with a simple warning. However, there was a day when I had on a bucket hat, army fatigue pants, and a tee shirt while I was going 5 mph above the speed limit. I was given a $90 ticket and questioned as to whether or not I had illegal items inside of my car.

It's unfortunate that I've been judged differently based off of my appearance, but from these occurrences, I determined that there is an opportunity in this opposition.

Surprisingly, the perception isn't only cast on you from the outside, but you actually influence your own attitude with what you wear. There was a study done at Yale University in 2014 in regards to how apparel can play a factor in your personal success.

"In a study completed at Yale in 2014 that used 128 men between the ages of 18 and 32, researchers had participants partake in mock negotiations of buying and selling. Those dressed poorly (in sweatpants and plastic sandals) averaged a theoretical profit of $680,000, while the group dressed in suits amassed an average profit of $2.1 million. The group dressed neutrally averaged a $1.58 million profit."

The concept of dressing the part for your brand or career will enhance your confidence in your daily executions. The feeling of professional imagery exudes a sense of power to the wearer of the garment and the person in contact with the professional.

Cloaked for The Pursuit

The purpose of taking care of your image won't just give you the results, but it grants you the opportunity to create more impact in your respective field.

I can recall in the transition from winter to spring in 2018, I went to a networking event in a brown cashmere suit with a unique vest. I arrived late and there weren't many people left at the event. So, I simply grabbed a few hors d'oeuvres from the beautiful palette on the table and munched away. Shortly after, someone complimented me on my apparel and sparked a conversation. She was astounded with my story and pulled me over to her group of friends to introduce me. We all had a conversation about a series of different topics. At the close of the evening, we exchanged contact information to remain connected.

A year passed by and one of the women contacted me about an opportunity to be the head of a department in her non-profit. She stated that she's been following me on social media consistently and loved seeing my growth, impact, and unique style. From there we have been able to build a quality relationship and connected with several different organizations nationwide to bring to our city.

I share that story because I want you to understand that this simply wouldn't have happened if I wasn't dressed the part at the networking event. I took the time out to value my appearance that day and from that, I was able to create a new meaningful relationship. All because of how I interacted with and them and the confidence that was exuded. Since I interacted with others effectively, they chose to follow me on social media platforms. Then, it gave them access to see more of my true character and yielded me a new opportunity. Your apparel is not going to close deals and make you an influential leader in your community—that is your job. Your apparel simply gives you a short window of time to capture the hearts and attention of others by standing out from the rest.

Now that you understand the importance of your image to the world, I need you to consider your personal brand. Yes, you are a brand.

Whether you are an entrepreneur or climbing the corporate ladder. With social media platforms being one of the main ways people define your character, you need to find your personal niche and what makes you stand distinct. Ask yourself, who are you and where are you going. As I just illustrated, your image grants you access to your future; define what the future looks like for you. Who you want to be will be significantly impacted by the way you dress.

If you are going to be a world-renowned event planner your style will likely include vibrant colors and unique patterns because you are a creative. If you want to be the new leader of the free world as President of the United States, then you may dress in power colors such as navy blue, white, and red. In every field there is a different form of dress. It is important that study it and then apply it.

Do not fall into the current trend of the billionaires that wear khakis and a white tee shirt. The reason they are able to do that is they have already achieved a high level of success. You, on the other hand, may have to still prove you are qualified to get to the next level of success. Even when you make it to where you desire to be, your industry may still require you to dress accordingly to create a consistent perception in your audience's eyes.

I know this book has and will continue to elevate your perspective. I am confident that it has enhanced your connection to God. Now that you have a stronger relationship, you can see what He has truly called you to be! If your closet doesn't reflect the vision God has given you, let's revamp it. You cannot continuously harbor old garments that are worn and torn. You can't wear an old thing to a new level. It doesn't reflect God's glory. He said that He would always keep you and that you will be a testimony for His people. So, why remain the same when you are destined to evolve into something greater?

So let's do this. When I sit down with prospective clients, I say...
"I want to be your personal clothier. My role is to help you continually develop your wardrobe in the direction where it is

Cloaked for The Pursuit

functional, quintessential, and producing quality results in your life."

At this very moment, you are an official client of Shaw's Covenant. I am going to give you the roadmap to develop your wardrobe. I will talk to you as if you have nothing in your closet. To start off, I want you to know that the role of any garment is to draw attention to the wearer's face. There are two factors that can achieve that; color and proportions.

Color

The colors for any ensemble should reflect the contrast of a person's skin & hair tones. There are three different categories you may fall under; medium contrast, high contrast, or mute contrast.

Medium Contrast

If you have a skin complexion that is close but not limited to a golden brown or caramel complexion with black hair, you would be defined as medium contrast. In this instance, you want to refrain from grouping monotone fabrics. If you are wearing a gray shirt/blouse with a brown jacket/skirt the contrast isn't deep enough to bring attention to your face. If you exchange the gray garment for a white garment it illuminates your face. It will brighten your white pupils and make your tan skin complexion lackluster.

High Contrast

If you have a very light skin tone and very dark hair, you want to be able to set a dynamic tone, because there is such a dynamic contrast. Don't be afraid to stay away from any monotone/earth colors. Your goal is to make beautiful contrasts. You can pair a dark color such as black (primary color) with a sky blue (secondary color) with a miscellaneous accent of white. I may be going overboard in the description, but just keep in mind that *your goal is a major contrast.*

MUTE COMPLEXION

Mute complexions have little to no contrast between their hair & skin. You may have very light skin, but your hair is blonde. The goal here is to not overpower your complexion with loud/noisy colors. You want to stick to warm colors to bring a warming complexion to your face. All earth tones are welcomed. You can wear dark colors, but they either have to be the accent color or be two-toned fabric, so the dark color will be washed out.

If you have any form of melanin in your skin (i.e. African American), you have the beauty of being either Medium or High Contrast.

PROPORTIONS

Proportion relies on your level of creativity. I may not be able to tell you all of the rules, but I will give you the surrounding guidelines that will help you understand it.

The goal of proportioning is to make your body look what is considered "normal". I highly encourage you to love your body the way it is; please know that I'm not saying your body isn't perfect. It's your clothing that is imperfect if they aren't custom made. You have to utilize your visual judgment to determine if a combination of garments proportion your body out evenly.

Tall	
Don't wear hats	It will make you taller
Don't wear stripes	Elongates your body
Cuff your sleeves/pants	It breaks up the length of your limbs
Longer Jackets/Shirts (Cover Your Seat)	It will make your torso & leg ratio even
Avoid Very Small-Scale Patterns (For Full Outfits)	It will be too much for the viewer's eye

Cloaked for The Pursuit

Short	
Don't Cuff sleeves/pants	It will make your limbs shorter
Welcomed to wear stripes	Elongates your body
Wear Hats	Increases your height
Shorter Cut Jackets/Shirts	It will lengthen your legs

Slim	
Have pockets/buttons on waist of jackets	It will fill your body shape out
Don't wear anything **too slim**	Distraction in Professional Environment & makes you look abnormally slim
Wear blouses/Tucked shirts with hang time (Women)	Creates larger hips (Hourglass shape)

Plus Size	
Wear Stripes	It will slim down your waistline
Less features on jackets/shirts	It will remove focus from torso
Be Careful with Bright Contrasting Colors	It will draw too much attention to the viewer's eye
Wear your pants above your waistline – Formal Wear (Men)	You do not want your stomach to hang over your pants. It compromises the clean drape of your garment

As I have stated before, these are just a few proportioning tips. Some of these fashion rules can be broken because it's based on the occasion, your specific body figure, and ultimately your preference and expression of creativity.

Finally, I want you to know the bare foundation of your entire wardrobe. This is very critical for versatility. Once you have these primary items you will be able to expand your wardrobe.

Men should have the following items:
- 2 White & 1 Blue Oxford Shirt
- Navy Blue & Charcoal Gray Suit
- 1 Pair of Jeans
- 2 Pair of Chinos (khaki & another color)
- Pair of Chestnut Dress shoes
- Pair of Brown Loafers
- Casual Shoes
- 4 Tee shirts

Women should have the following items:
- 1 White & 1 Blue Oxford Shirt
- 2-3 Blouses
- Navy Blue & Charcoal Gray/Black Suits
- 1 /Any Color Jacket
- 3-4 Dresses
- Black & Nude Heels
- 3 Pair of Flats
- 1 Pair of Tennis Shoes
- 2 Skirts (at or below the knee)
- 4 Tee Shirts
- 1 pair of Jeans

As Christians, we are a reflection of God's love. You've come this far through your trials & tribulations and He has still kept you! You are a prize in His eyes. Until you decide to view yourself as one of His children, not only in a mental capacity but physically, you will limit the expansion of your purpose.

There is a story in the bible (Luke 15:11-24) about a son that lived his life wildly. He left his father's land with his inheritance and spoiled it. He became a servant of others in another country. He was living in famine as he labored over a pigsty. He realized that his father's servants were never ill-fed, so he ventured back home. When his father saw, him coming, he ran to him with compassion and the son cried to him, "I am no longer worthy to be called your son; make me like one of your hired servants." The father called his

Cloaked for The Pursuit
servants to cloak his son in the best robe along with a ring & pair of sandals. They prepared a feast in the returning of the son as he was cloaked with the best garments for his renewed life!

So many of us make the common mistake of straying away from our connection with God the Father and feel ashamed for coming back. What we choose not to understand is that He is the constant in our life that will forever run back to us and cover us with the best robe and hide our splinters with sandals. You are a representation of God's Glory. Yes, we have all been through a mess, we all experience doubt and fear on our journeys. But when we are connected to the Father, we won't look like what we have gone through.

I am passionate about apparel because it has helped shape me into the eternal purpose God has designed for me. It has been able to distinguish me from the rest of the crowd. I've been strategically placed by God in certain environments, because of my obedience and my testimony.

When they see you, they will be astounded by your accomplishments, but blessed by your testimony. Your clothes don't make you who you are, your story does. Ensure that you have cloaked yourself with the appropriate garments for your pursuit to purpose because you will be a beacon of light for those that need to see in the dark. Your pursuit is connected to someone else's blessing, so utilize your gifts and talents to produce fruit and plant seeds on good ground. I pray that when others see you, they see God's Glory.

JUSTIN SHAW

Justin Shaw, born in Baltimore Maryland wasn't always considered the most fashion forward character in his younger years. But as time progressed he had the opportunity to finally exercise his fashion sense once he became a young adult. What started as a simple form of expression turned into a passion.

He was known as an entrepreneur in the Maryland marketplace, but had a knack for catching the eye of anyone who caught sight of his appearance. After meditating for months, he had a revelation to start his own Clothier. He didn't want to just start a company for profit, but for impact. He believes that your appearance is inevitably the gateway to your performance and your presence.

Website:
www.shawscovenant.com

Cloaked for The Pursuit

9. Emerge

IN YOUR FINANCES; BREAK FREE FROM BAD CREDIT

Ronda Brunson

How ironic is it that I was asked to participate in the writing of this book at such a time as this; with a lunatic in the White House and 800,000 federal workers out of work and struggling to make ends meet. This reminds me of how important it is to be proactive instead of reactive. The old folks used to say, "If you stay ready you don't have to get ready"

Remember when the goal was to graduate school and get a "good government job"? Now, not so much. With almost a million people not receiving paychecks due to a government shutdown, one must wonder what happens to their bills. I do applaud the nonprofits and private citizens that have stepped up to assist. We all should do something to help our brothers and sisters experiencing this crisis. This situation teaches us a valuable lesson on living like there IS a tomorrow.

Break Free From Bad Credit

Now I already know when it comes to discussing credit, sometimes people are tempted to walk in shame and condemnation about their failures, mistakes and the reality of where you are. I want you to release that shame and guilt now and know that everything shared in this chapter is to empower you to make better choices and create a better tomorrow. *"My people are destroyed for a lack of knowledge."* Hosea 4:6. What you don't know about credit can cause financial ruin. So be encouraged this chapter is here to bring life!

I'm not going to bore you with the utilization and usage rules that you have heard day in and day out. I don't have any new information that relates to that. I will instead encourage you to begin applying them since we don't know what to expect from day to day. I'm sure none of these folks with "good government jobs" would have ever expected to experience such a lengthy furlough. I will also encourage you to create that emergency savings account that we all desire to have yet less than 30% of us actually do. How can I save when I have no money? First, analyze your outgo and audit your bank accounts. I highly encourage financial journals especially for those who make the money but never feel like they have enough to make ends meet. The first place I would look would be habits and food. So many of us market and eat out which can become wasteful. Cut out the fat literally and take the trimmings to the bank

Your behavior matters!

The primary reason people schedule appointments with me is to learn how they can improve their credit score. In my counseling sessions, I turn that question back on them and ask "well how can we improve your behavior"?

Your credit report is a document that displays how well you manage debt. The score is your grade. In my office, we don't focus on the score but the content and integrity of the report while teaching that debt and credit are two totally different things that work together. A person with a 600 can be approved for many things while the person with the 800 can be denied. There are all types of factors considered when applying for credit such as Income, Credit history, and Length of employment.

If the person with a 600 goes to a lending institution with high debt (not necessarily high balances) yet everything has been current for 3 years or longer if their income allows they can be approved for what they are requesting BUT possibly at a higher APR The person with an 800 can go and apply for the same loan type and be denied. Here's why. Let's say the score is 800 but the credit file itself hasn't been active in over 24 months. The scores froze where they last were and the history remained intact but is no longer relevant. It's like a stamp on the report. This person could be turned away due to lack of active credit history or subjected to a higher APR than someone who has been paying a lot of credit accounts for years on time

Think fast! Are you a Transactor or a Revolver?

A few years back these phrases were introduced to the world of credit as a means to categorize a consumer's behavior

A transactor is a person who swipes $500 in a credit card and paying $500 back when the statement arrives in full. A Revolver is a person who swipes $500.00 and sends a little over the monthly payment each month for the next year or so still swiping from time to time carrying balances forever. Transactions benefit from higher approval ratings and lower interest rates while Revolvers are subjected to higher APRs paying 10x more for the same car as another person because they are higher risk.

Which are you? Change your behavior, change your life!

Now we always claim that we want the best, but when the being the best requires sacrifice we often cringe and throw in the towel. Your credit scores are directly related to how consistent and dependable you. They also account for the amount of risk you display. Scores, however, don't guarantee approvals. Approvals are determined by underwriters and the sole question they are asking is "how likely is this person to repay?"

So what does your report say about you? Would you lend you money? Do you exhibit all of the behaviors of a consumer that can be trusted?

1- PAY ALL BILLS ON TIME.

"I forgot" is not an adequate response for making a late payment. You can use autopay through most creditors' sites and also through your own online bill pay to ensure payments are made on time. Understand that late payments come with consequences and can set your scores back 6-10 months. Too many late payments will cause future lenders to see you as undependable and an easy target for a higher interest rate the next time.

2- DON'T BE THIRSTY

A fun analogy I like to use with my clients and on seminars is this:

Imagine if you and I have been friends for a little while and I need to use your car. You agree but give me restrictions. "Ronda, you can use my car but you can only go about 10 minutes up the street to the mall". I agree, but I get into your car and realize there's a tank full of gas and navigation and a great stereo system. I'm excited. I decide I'm taking this car to the mall furthest away. Six hours later I show up and I'm feeling good. I filled the tank back up. I found everything I needed at the mall. I pull up in your driveway and you are fuming! I can't understand. I mean you said you had nothing to do that day what's the big deal.

This is what my clients have done with their credit cards in the past. They have taken them on a ride. Keeping high utilization and simply paying the minimum each month. Don't be that friend! Follow the rules of credit. Use little and repay most monthly. This is how you will improve your scores and impress banks and entice them into rewarding your behavior.

3 - FORGIVE YOURSELF

Imagine if you were as forgiving of yourself as credit agencies are of you.

I recently spoke to a young lady who had disputed the account status on a charged off capital one account which hadn't updated since 2015. When she sent me the message through my direct messenger on Instagram I immediately asks for her number and called and shouted; "Who told you to do that!"

"Well, Ms. Ronda I settled that account and it shouldn't be on my report anymore" I probed, "says who?" She continued "I thought that if I had paid it, it would go away."

I rebutted with a really random yet relevant question "How many ex-boyfriends have you had?" She replied "4". I continued, "As much as you may have disliked some of the things that have caused you to now be 'exes' or all of the ways they hurt you or got under your skin... the reality is you cannot delete them. They are a factual part of your past. Your relationship is over but what you learned from each experience is still valuable."

She paused. The light bulb was starting to shine a little brighter

"But If you look at the wording, it's saying that I refused to pay but I paid in 2018"

I laughed a little to myself and countered with this "let's say that you gave me $500 in my hand with the understanding that I was going to repay all $500 in 30 days. Here we are 3 years later and I still haven't paid you - would that not be a refusal?"

"Ohhhh but I disputed it and it dropped my scores" "Yes! Because you made them reinvestigate an issue that hasn't been all that relevant since 2015!" Are you following me?

4 - SET REASONABLE EXPECTATIONS

Life happens which can cause us to fall victim to late pays, evictions, repossessions, charge offs etc. All of these things are a part of your history. They do not define who you are now or who you will be. During the credit rebuilding process, you will need to pace yourself. Your scores don't go from 500 to 700 in 12 months. Sometimes not even 24 months. You must allow time to heal old wounds, implement new behaviors and remember to celebrate the small increases along the way.

5 - PERFECTION IS A GOAL, NOT A NECESSITY AS IT RELATES TO APPROVABILITY.

Nowhere on any application does it say that your credit has to be perfect to qualify. In fact, even with a few small blemishes, you can qualify for a home, personal loan, car, credit cards, and the list goes on. The banks and bureaus are not focused on your fall but how you recovered. We fall down but we get up through the grace of God.

The past holds you but the future frees you. Grab your new tools and begin painting a better, healthier, less risky credit picture today. Break free of the guilt and shame of the mistakes you've made in the past. Be grateful for second, third, fourth and even fifth chances. You are in complete control and there is always an opportunity to get back on track. You've got this! I believe in you

RONDA BRUNSON

Ronda Brunson, also known as Ms. B Credit Queen, is a credit restoration specialist who has helped countless people reclaim their lives through building of strong credit. She is a board member for the National Association of Credit Counselors. She is also the visionary behind Project Restore Bmore, a non-profit dedicated to assisting minorities with homeownership. She is a choice council member of Women By Choice a global women's empowerment organization and s a speaker for their annual cruise in Cuba. Her writing has been featured in Heart & Soul magazine.

Website:
https://msbcreditqueen.com

Break Free From Bad Credit

10. EMERGE

IN STEWARDSHIP: LIFE ON A BUDGET

Taryn Bushrod

Finances and budgets are two words that can strike a chord, but money has a very different connotation for different people. Money is a universal language that every human understands. It varies in color, size, and types of paper/metal but the question "how much" is always followed by a price. Whether it's paid in dollars, pesos or euros or with cash, credit or digital currency; money is how we pay for what we want in life. The bible tells us in Ecclesiastes 10:19 that *"money answers all things"*. Money is the economic resource that gives us the ability to do or buy what we want when we have it in excess, but it can also be limiting if do we do not have enough or as much as we desire. How much money we currently have access to determines our buying power. There are levels to money and access varying from poverty to wealth. Then there is classism, everyone has a place in society that is highly impacted by their access to money. Elevating yourself to the next level is often determined by your ability to increase and manage your cash flow. Stewardship is a key component to achieving the changes you desire in your finances.

You may be asking yourself what does it mean to be a good steward. Stewardship is defined as "conducting, supervising, or managing something." This can be translated into something as simple as taking care of your money. Have you heard the phrase "Pay Yourself First" or more importantly "Pay God First?" This is where your journey to becoming a good steward over your finances begins. By developing a good relationship with money, you will enable yourself to take control of your money. Paying God or yourself first is a level of commitment that is an indicator of good money management. Through this process, you will be able to identify your spending habits, triggers and assess your values surrounding money. A good relationship with money will help you avoid common pitfalls such as buying a new car, house or clothes when you receive a lump sum of money such as a refund from overpaying taxes. Often times these desires to upgrade our lifestyle are driven by music, entertainment, social media and essentially all forms of advertising. This is a prime example of the behavioral mindset that influences your spending referred to as consumerism.

Having a desire to change your lifestyle with a monetary increase is not uncommon yet a good steward will learn to practice delayed gratification and manage well what they currently have. There is power in acknowledging that you want something and you are willing to wait by saving for it first. Learning to control your impulses can save you a lot of money and heartache. You avoid the use of credit cards which will save you money in interest and the item could be on sale by the time you reach your savings goal. You can also learn what it means to invest now and spend later. There is always a tradeoff between impulse spending and delayed gratification. When you are faced with buying decisions, consider what you are depriving your future self of having. Your impulse decisions have a domino effect on other aspects of your life. It can cause you to miss out on a life-changing investment opportunity or fall into debt for something as small as an auto repair. Each day you have an opportunity to make certain sacrifices that will grant you a better life in the future. Your buying decisions should shift after you ask yourself how much is my future self-worth.

Currently, there is a paradigm shift surrounding consumer behavior. Especially, in communities of color. More people are speaking out to change the narrative of consumerism and educate others towards becoming conscious consumers. Education is the basis of change in anything we do. The more informed someone is the greater their chances are of making better decisions and better decisions leads to being a good steward over our finances.

As a money coach, the phrase I hear the most is "I don't know where my money is going." This is a common issue many people face that starts by not knowing the exact amount of money they make on a monthly basis or the total amount of their living expenses. Without knowing these two numbers it's impossible to effectively manage your money. Knowing your payday is not enough to break the vicious cycle of living paycheck to paycheck. You must establish a plan to take control of your money. This is where the "B-Word" comes into play, a BUDGET. Depending upon how you view budgeting, it can be your best friend or your worst nightmare. If you think it's restricting then you can expect to struggle with sticking to your budget. I challenge you to view a budget in its simplest form. That it tells your money where to go. If you don't tell your money where to go it will run away from you as fast as you get it. Implementing small changes such as solely using cash won't help you if you don't start with a budget. Yet, all budgets aren't created equal. Aside from everyone having different amounts of money, it's also about the varying views and interactions with money. The process that works best for you could cause someone else to mismanage their funds which stresses the importance of determining a system that works best for you. Whether it's the perfect money tracking apps such as Personal Capital or Qapital, a personalized excel spreadsheet or pen and paper. If you want to stay on top of your money find your system and actually implement it.

Life On A Budget

Furthermore, you could have conflicting views about money. If your views align with the You Only Live Once (Y.O.L.O.) philosophy very prevalent amongst millennials, you are more inclined to spend money and treat yourself without consulting your budget. While someone who aspires to join what the finance community calls F.I.R.E. which stands for Financially Independent, Retire Early, they will exercise delayed gratification. These philosophies are on opposite sides of the money management spectrum with varying uses for money. This is why I suggested understanding your relationship with money.

To take a deeper dive you can start by asking yourself three questions.

- What was your very first encounter with money?
- What is your most memorable experience with money?
- Currently, how does money make you feel?

Now ask yourself if you are a mindless spender or relentless saver and investor. These questions will help you start the process of unlocking your money persona. This insight will enhance your budgeting experience and give you a better idea of where to start and where you want to tell your money to go.

If your goals are more complex, if they extend beyond the basics of budgeting, and you want to design a lifestyle where you can save/invest, pay off debt, and still have some fun, then I recommend a money management plan such as the 50/20/30 rule. The 50 is for your living essentials which shouldn't exceed 50 percent of your cash flow, 20 percent is for your financial goals such as savings/investing and debt repayment. The 30 percent is the golden key to your "fun fund." This is the amount you can use for flexible spending. The monthly brunches, happy hours, date nights or traveling all fall within the 30 percent threshold. The secret to managing money is to plan in advance and forecast as much as you can. Your money will go a lot further and you'll maintain more control. You also want to refresh your numbers every month. Perhaps you use the entire 30 percent this month but your forecast for next month indicates you'll only use 20 percent. You want to ensure you capture the remaining 10 percent and increase your savings or add it to your debt repayment. This is another way you can keep your money from running away from you.

I began learning money principles as a kid. The very first lesson came from my grandfather as soon as I learned how to count. He taught me to save a nickel of every dollar no matter what and when he gave me money it would be in coins to ensure I put five cents in my piggy bank. Along with this lesson, he taught me the importance of saving. The difference in having savings and not having savings can drastically impact your quality of life. Having savings gives you options and my grandfather made sure I had plenty of options by giving me a savings bond for every birthday, Christmas gift or special occasion. When I was in elementary school he took me to open my first bank account at Baltimore County Savings Bank. I remember giving him money to deposit into my account every week. I got so much joy from seeing my balance increase month to month. Even at an early age, I believe this sense of achievement from learning to save gave me a greater appreciation for money. Needless to say, I learned how to be responsible with money at a very young age as my grandfather was a stickler for managing money.

Eventually, he gave me dollar bills when it came time to give me money to put into the offering basket at church. And he watched closely to make sure I didn't keep any of it for myself. This was my earliest teaching of "Pay God First." By this time I was in Middle School. This principle helped me develop discipline as it wasn't necessarily what I wanted to do with the money I was given. I wanted to spend my money on toys and candy like most kids and sometimes I did just that. However, I quickly realized I didn't want to use my money for candy and toys. I'd rather have other people buy it for me and save my money for unknown desires in the future.

Life On A Budget

On my journey to adulting, I had encounters that contradicted the money principles I was taught as a child. I've experienced consumerism, credit card debt and not having any savings. Some of it stemmed from a loss of income while others were just growing pains but hard decisions had to be made. Once I decided to make giving and saving a priority, all the feelings I felt as a kid came rushing back to me. This feeling transformed me as I fully understood the more money you have the more you can help others and my determination to meet my objectives intensified. I believe financial education is the greatest investment we can make in ourselves and it all points back to being a good steward and living by a budget.

TARYN BUSHROD

Taryn Bushrod is a 2018 Forbes Fellow and Baltimore native who graduated from Morgan State University with a Bachelor's of Science degree in Marketing. She went on to receive a Master's of Science degree in Financial Management while working as a Contract Specialist for the Defense Logistics Agency. She currently resides in Washington, DC and works in the Finance and Budget Division for the Department of Homeland Security.

Her journey to becoming a Money Coach began at an early age with the teachings of sound money principles from her Father and Grandfather. After years of helping friends and family manage their funds she decided it was time to help others learn what she had learned on a broader spectrum. In 2017, Taryn launched a platform to help millennials understand their relationship with money and spending habits so they can take control of their finances and create a life that doesn't break the bank.

She is a proud member of Delta Sigma Theta Sorority, Inc. and takes pride in helping others thrive by taking control of their finances and increasing their financial wellness.

Website:
www.tarynsworld.com

Life On A Budget

11. EMERGE

IN YOUR WEALTH PRINCIPLES.
YOU WERE CREATED TO PROSPER!

Constance Craig-Mason

If you are anything like me, you didn't grow up with a silver spoon in your mouth. As a matter of fact, I was born and raised in the inner city of Baltimore, MD to a young, single mom. If I can be completely transparent, we lived in unstable home environments, impoverished, witnessing domestic violence and substance abuse. I watched my mother struggle to retain stable work, provide adequate means of the basic necessities and try to improve herself personally and professionally. She was ignorant concerning "how money works". Therefore, the "American Dream" of the nice home with the white picket fence, with the 2-car garage and 2.5 children was certainly out of reach for her and for us. You can't teach what you don't know, right?

Experiencing the effects of inheriting financial illiteracy fueled me to seek more for my life. But where would I start? I mean, you don't

You Were Created To Prosper

know what you don't know, until you know it! As I stumbled through my latter teenage years as a young, single mom myself, I became so frustrated. The constant let downs, turn downs and disappointments were all too encompassing. I had no idea who I was, what my purpose was and to be honest where our next meal was coming from. But I knew there was a God and if I could just get to know Him better, maybe He could change some things. I mean, it couldn't get much worse than being a victim of molestation, abuse, depression, loneliness, poverty, and single-motherhood all by the age of 21, right?

My desire to learn more about God also led me to discovering more about myself. I was super excited to learn who He was, how He feels about me and His desires for my life. See, I had an identity crisis. I'm sure I am not the only one who experienced the ill-effects of not knowing who and whose I was. From reading the Bible, I learned that from the very beginning, God and His Word are the same. And that He created everything, including me (John 1:1-3). There was no accident, nor circumstance that caused me to walk this earth. As a matter of fact, when I read that I am not only a child of God but an heir, I couldn't believe my eyes (Galatians 4:6-7). But how could an "heir" be broke and broken? I was confused, but I kept reading!

Not only had He created me, He knew me before I was even formed in my mom's belly (Jeremiah 1:5). And He had already made plans to prosper me, give me hope and a future (Jeremiah 29:11). Can you imagine the stark difference between what I was reading, what I felt and what I saw in my reality? Conflicted, but I kept reading! Even better yet, was when I found out that not only did He want me to be successful, but He would give me the ability (power) to get wealth (Deuteronomy 8:18)! Me? With my family history, background, circumstances, etc.? Yup, so much so that He sent His Son, with all His principles and His Spirit with all of His wisdom to make sure that I have a full, abundant life (John 10: 10, John 14:26).

He took away all of my excuses, confusion, and doubt. But now, I had to get to work! Doing what? I literally and spiritually had to

A.S.K. Ask and it shall be given. Seek and find. Knock and the door will be opened (Matthew 7:7). Actually, this scripture was so pivotal in my life, it was the foundation for the business consulting company that I established years later called, ASK Business Consulting Services, LLC. In the practical sense, I used that principle to continuously seek out financial literacy that would forever change my life. It was the catalyst for the shift that fuels my passion & purpose to help others.

After years of working jobs that seemingly didn't "feel" anything like what I thought passion and purpose should feel like, I found it! Actually, I had been unofficially doing it outside of work. As I was navigating through life, figuring things out and turning losses into lessons, I started sharing what I was learning with those in my circle. You know, family, friends, coworkers. Ok, even strangers I struck up conversations with on the bus. Don't judge me! I was super excited about what was working for me, so how could I keep it to myself?

Everything from budgeting to credit, savings, insurance, investing, mortgage loans, real estate investing, you name it. I read EVERYTHING! My girlfriend, who was working in the financial services field, suggested that I join her in the profession. She said, "You do this anyway. Why don't you get licensed, share what you know and earn income from it?" It took almost 7 years for me to take her up on it, because I had limited daycare options. But a few years after I got married, I jumped in and went full speed ahead! It was my first successful experience with entrepreneurship, which was a chain-breaker for my family. Helping others break the chains of financial illiteracy was not just something cute to say. I was living it and teaching it simultaneously!

Financial literacy is when you have the knowledge and skill sets that allow you to make informed and effective decisions with your resources. But as a movement, it helps to promote "financial wellness", which refers to your overall financial health. **Financial well-being** is a state of being where a person can fully meet current

You Were Created To Prosper

and ongoing obligations, feel secure in their financial future and is able to make choices that allow them to enjoy life. Sounds fancy, huh? In layman's terms, it's having financial security and freedom of choice now and in the future. Pretty dope, right? Well, let me tell you about another dope movement! It's called FIRE and it stands for **Financial Independence, Retire Early!** The goal of this movement is accumulating a sufficient amount of wealth, as quickly as possible. However, how would you know how much is "sufficient" for you to be able to live your best-retired life earlier? Well, in order to find your "wealth number," you can multiply your annual spending (not your annual income) by 25. Then, multiply that amount by 4%, which is the annual amount you will have to live.

ANNUAL SPENDING (AMOUNT TO LIFE ON) X 25 = WEALTH NUMBER

Let us try it! Suppose your annual spending is roughly $36,000. Multiply that by 25; it equals $900,000. That is the amount you need to retire with F.I.R.E, withdrawing $36,000 (4%) to live on each year! You might be thinking, "How am I supposed to save nearly a million dollars in a short amount of time?" My friend, the short answer is financial integrity. It's when your daily actions align with the financial principles you've learned and the financial plans you've made.

Well, what is one of those financial principles? **The Wealth Formula** is a crucial one to understand. It is effortless; when understood and implemented, it can change the course of your entire financial life! Are you ready for it?

WEALTH = MONEY + TIME +/- RATE OF RETURN - INFLATION – TAXES

The money that I am referring to are the funds that you deposit into an account for long term savings. For example, your employer may allow you to select a percentage or set amount of your paycheck to direct towards a 401k, 403b or similar account. You will need to be consistent with those fund deposits over time. The longer you keep the account, the more those funds get exposed to a rate of return. Depending on the type of retirement account you elect, the rate of return, can fluctuate or be fixed. You will want to speak with a Certified Financial Planner (CFP) regarding the best option for you.

Inflation is expressed as the rate of which the cost of goods and services are going up, and the purchasing power of the dollar is going down. Each year it costs more money to buy the same goods and services as the year before. Inflation has averaged about 3% in the US, over the last 100 years! Moreover, again, depending on what type of retirement account you have, taxes on the funds may be deferred or tax-free. In a nutshell, you build wealth when you can consistently invest, gaining an interest rate that offsets inflation and taxes!

Do you want me to share another financial principle? Of course, you do! Have you heard of compound interest before? The great Albert Einstein said "Compound interest is the eighth wonder of the world. He who understands it earns it. He who does not pay it." Wow? Compound interest is also known as a formula called **The Rule of 72**. This formula determines how long it takes for your investment to double, based on a given fixed annual rate of return. "English, please!"

72 / RATE OF RETURN = # OF YEARS TO DOUBLE

For example, if you deposited $1,000 into your retirement account, without adding any additional funds to it. Also, the fixed annual rate of return is 3%. Based on The Rule of 72, you would divide 72 by 3. That equals 24. That means that it would take 24 years for that initial deposit of $1,000 to double to $2,000. That is a long time to wait to earn just $1,000 more, right? Well, what if the interest rate earned was higher than 3%? Let us try an 8% annual rate of return. 72 divided by 8 equals 9. So that initial deposit of $1,000 doubles to $2,000 in just 9 years. I like that way better! You just learned that money doubles quicker when you earn a higher interest rate, right?

You Were Created To Prosper
Yes! I know, I know! Now, you want to know where you can get the best interest rates on your retirement accounts. My recommendation is that you speak with a Certified Financial Planner (CFP), who is licensed to go over all the best options for your risk tolerance, time frame, budget and wealth number.

Your understanding of the Wealth Formula and The Rule of 72 should give you the motivation to set your retirement on F.I.R.E! So, FIRE-starter, allow me to share some practical tips on where to focus your efforts. You will need to do a **Personal Finance Assessment (PFA)**. A PFA will include listing the value of your assets (what you own) and the amount of your liabilities (what you owe). Assets represent the amount of cash, investments, the market value of real estate, vehicles, jewelry or anything you own of value. Add those up. Then, calculate the amount of debt that you owe on those assets and other debts. Subtract the total amount of your assets from the total amount of your liabilities. The resulting number is your **net worth**. Ideally, you want your net worth to be a positive number, not a negative number. If it is negative, that means you owe more than you own. *I will touch on that later in this chapter.*

A PFA will also include a **personal budget or spending plan** for those of us who gag at the idea of the word budget! You will list your estimated monthly net income (what you earn) and expenses (what you spend). This will be quite simple if you have fixed expenses such as rent or a mortgage. However, keep in mind, you should list the average amount that you spend on variable expenses such as groceries, gas, utilities, etc. You can easily find this info on your bank or credit card statements. I recommend reviewing the last 3 months to determine your average for those. Subtract the total amount of your monthly net income from the total amount of your monthly expenses. The resulting number is your **cash flow**. If you come up short, you will need to address this sooner rather than later. *I will touch on that later in this chapter also!* Positive cash flow is an indicator of living within your means and the availability of funds for short term emergencies, long term investing, future projects or goals.

If you find that you have a positive monthly cash flow, be sure to set aside some of that money for emergencies. Set up an **emergency account** targeting at least 3-6 months of expenses. Considering the fact that it takes the average unemployed worker about 4 months to secure a job, it is critical to prioritize saving. It may take some time to accumulate that amount, but consistency is critical. In December 2018, approximately 800,000 federal workers experienced a furlough, where they were required to work or stay at home without pay for nearly 35 days. So the loss of government assistance affected millions more. It became the longest federal government shutdown in history. Do you think those who had enough emergency savings were able to keep food on their tables, utilities on, gas in their vehicles, etc.? I do it! If you struggle with tracking your spending or saving consistently, reach out for help. A Financial Coach is a professional, who specializes in teaching how money works & developing healthy money habits, money management, spending plans and is an accountability partner on your journey towards positive financial well-being.

If you owe more than you own or if you spend more than you earn, these can be holding you back from accumulating the wealth you need to live your best-retired life! You can address those issues in a couple of ways. Beef up your human capital! What in the world is that? Invest in yourself in ways that potentially increase your earning potential. Find free or minimal cost certificate programs such as Coursera, LearnThat.com, FutureLearn.com, iTunes U to advance your skillsets and position you to qualify for promotions or higher paying opportunities elsewhere. You can also seek out additional income earning opportunities, such as a part-time job or turn a hobby into a business.

Use the extra income to accelerate paying down (or off) your debt. *Side note: By doing so, you will also increase or improve your credit score and demonstrate financial integrity to your existing creditors.* Do not forget to throw some of that extra income into your emergency savings account, so that you can reach your goal of 3-6 months stashed away. I would also recommend reviewing your spending plan for the areas you can reduce costs. For example, do you really watch 330+ channels a month? Have you been a loyal customer to the cable company? Call them and see if they can reduce your monthly bill by applying loyalty credits or promos. Alternatively, tell them the channels that you watch and let find you a less expensive package that still suits your viewing pleasure. You like that don't you? I did not say you had to give it up! Do the same with your utility providers and cell phone carrier. Shop around for a better rate, without sacrificing the quality of service.

Call your insurance agent and ask for an **insurance review** of your auto, home and life policies. You would be surprised at the amount of premium savings that are available to you, just by asking! Mitigating risk and liability allows you to keep more of the income you earn. In the unfortunate event of disability or death of a breadwinner, income replacement is critical to lifestyle sustainability. Also, it may be beneficial to contact a Certified Public Accountant (CPA), not necessarily the chick who does your taxes at the mall, to see if there are ways to reduce your tax liability. There could be withholdings that need adjusting on your W4 at work that could put you in a position to bring home more net pay, without owing the IRS the following year. Also, there could be tax credits that you are entitled to that you are not aware of that could increase the amount of your tax refund.

I encourage you to pursue, what I call a Financial Dream Team. These are licensed, experienced professionals in various areas of the financial industry that can make themselves available to answer your questions and assist you when needed. I mentioned a few of them in this chapter, such as a Financial Coach, Certified Financial Planner (CFP), Certified Public Accountant (CPA) and Insurance Agent. I did not previously state this but seek out an excellent Personal Banker also. These are professionals at your local banks, who specialize in helping you with managing your daily money matters. They can help review your accounts to reduce any unnecessary fees, dispute unauthorized charges and make the best use of the bank as a resource.

Do not try to wing it, when it comes to establishing, protecting and increasing your wealth. Outsourcing to experts may cost you some money, but not nearly as much as ignorance could. Financial freedom is the 21st-century definition of retirement, meaning that you can maintain your desired lifestyle without a regular paycheck. Tag you are it! The first one to financial freedom wins!

CONSTANCE CRAIG-MASON

Constance Craig-Mason is a passionate International Speaker, experienced Licensed Insurance Broker, dedicated Financial Coach and former Small Business Consultant. She has been helping individuals, families and businesses for over 10 years. Licensed in Maryland and Pennsylvania, she has been blessed to have worked some of the top insurance carriers to include Transamerica, State Farm, Baltimore Life and Primerica. Constance provides a full Complimentary Financial Analysis that includes spending plan, short & long term savings, credit restoration, debt elimination, insurance protection & retirement supplement strategies. As a Financial Coach, Constance works with her clients to develop realistic strategies that reflect their current needs and future goals, periodically following up to make sure that they are making positive strides and re-assesses, if things have changed.

Website:
www.tanconnects.com/ccraigmason

WHAT'S NEXT?

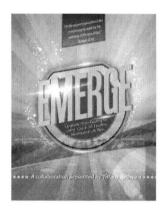

Looking for more? If this book has impacted you and you are looking for more visit the book website for additional resources and events to continue your EMERGE journey.

Share your reflections on social media and be sure to use the hashtag **#emergebook** so we can repost and interact with you.

Visit www.emergethebook.com for more.

43097054R00060

Made in the USA
Middletown, DE
23 April 2019